FINAL EMPIRE

Religious Liberty's Last Stand

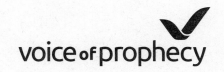

voice of prophecy

and Pacific Press Publishing Association

Cover Illustration by Palmer Halvorson
Cover and Interior Design by Mark Bond
Text Typeset: Minion Pro

Additional copies of *Final Empire,* resources mentioned in this book's
footnotes, and many other spiritual resources are available by calling
toll-free 1-844-822-2943 or by visiting vop.com/store.

Printed in the United States of America by
Pacific Press Publishing Association, Nampa, Idaho.

www.pacificpress.com

ISBN: 978-1-9429-9731-3

Contents

A Note to the Reader:

When I first set out to write this little book, I envisioned a much larger, more comprehensive volume—many hundreds of pages in length. The topic it deals with—the rise of the American republic and its place in the prophetic scheme of the Bible—is a subject that has commanded a great deal of my time and attention during the last nearly three decades. I may still produce a much fuller book in the future, God willing. The rigors of a production schedule and the need to keep this book affordable and easy to distribute in connection with the 2020 *Final Empire* event, however, have made it necessary to provide a much less ambitious work for the time being.

Consider this book an outline intended to prompt further study. It is my prayer that while you will certainly not find all the answers you seek in this little volume, you *will* find enough to stir a desire to explore history as it relates to Bible prophecy more deeply for yourself.

Additionally, you will notice that some of the chapters are longer than others. I debated trying to equalize them, but to do so seemed artificial and unnecessary. In a generation where all stories are told in either twenty-eight or fifty-eight minutes, it is important to remember: not all stories can be told that neatly.

Shawn Boonstra

Introduction

Years ago there was a rather clever show on the BBC called *Connections.* There were only ever ten episodes, but the premise was sufficiently brilliant that I have often regretted there weren't more. The host, James Burke, would choose some seemingly random event from the distant past—say, the invention of the stirrup—and then trace his way through a long chain of historical events to the present, showing how that random event eventually gave rise to a scientific development in the present, such as the atomic bomb.

It takes a lot to get me hooked on a TV show; I would much rather read a book. But *Connections* was irresistible. *Of course,* I had to know how, without the stirrup, there would never have been an A-bomb! One might argue, of course, that by starting in the present and working your way back, it becomes an easy task to connect two distant events. All you have to do is stop moving your way down the chain of history when you find something interesting and seemingly random—and presto! You have the makings of a show.

Far more impressive than working your way back is starting in the present and accurately predicting the future—a skill that James Burke also seemed to possess. In 1973, he predicted that the human race was headed for an age of information when computers would be widespread and people would be willing to divulge huge swaths of personal information to perfect strangers. Witness the rise of Facebook, where roughly one third of the earth's population happily puts their entire lives on display for whomever might like to see it.

Burke's prediction was more accurate than even he understood at the time. He didn't envision social media, exactly: he was speaking about using computers for business applications, and predicted there would be 300,000 computer terminals in use by the year 2000. He was wrong by tens of millions: we *all* own computers, and they are all far more advanced than the terminals he envisioned. It was an impressive prediction nonetheless. James Burke has a gift for anticipating where scientific and technological trends might lead; when a prediction gets close, we are all duly impressed. Nobody expects the prognostications of futurists to be 100 percent accurate. If they were, we would have to wonder if someone had covertly invented a time machine.

The future is notoriously difficult to predict, because even slight variations in events today can have huge ramifications even a few years down the road. Half a century ago Edward Lorenz, the famous meteorologist, raised a now-famous question at a symposium: "Does the flap of a butterfly's wings in Brazil set off a tornado in Texas?"[1] The point he was making is that intertwined systems are far too complex for anybody to accurately predict future outcomes. Change one small detail in the present or get one of your measurements wrong, and down the road the results will vary dramatically from your meagerly-informed predictions. None of us possesses a sufficient data set to enable us to predict everything with any degree of certainty.

Some refer to this as *chaos theory,* the idea that the universe is orderly and theoretically predictable, but there are too many random factors at play for limited human intelligence to reliably accomplish this. It's an idea that challenges one of the key

---

1   Jamie L. Vernon, "Understanding the Butterfly Effect," *American Scientist,* May–June 2017.

concepts that came out of the Enlightenment: the universe as a *machine*. As the world moved from medieval to modern times, we began to view the cosmos as a finely-tuned machine with predictable outcomes. We convinced ourselves that we could master our environment through observation and reason. It was a useful idea, because it yielded an impressive number of advancements, including electricity, global communications, and modern medicine.

But then we turned our attention to the world of the incredibly small. Quantum mechanics yielded a disturbing discovery: the subatomic world does not appear to work by the same set of physical laws as the larger universe. In 1927, Werner Heisenberg noticed that by simply *observing* a subatomic particle you would change its behavior, making it utterly impossible to obtain a simultaneous measurement by a second scientist.[2] The more accurately the position of the particle can be recorded, the less certain you become about its velocity, and vice versa. His discovery is now called the *uncertainty principle,* and it highlights just how random the world of the very small seems to be.

We don't *like* random. We want predictability.

Enter Erwin Schroedinger, who produced a fascinating thought experiment in 1935. Because the very act of observation can change the outcome of an event, he argued that it is impossible to know exactly what might happen in any given instance. He created a metaphor to explain what he meant.

---

2 This discovery has yielded some very strange possibilities indeed—
   including, according to some speculative articles I've stumbled across,
   the possibility that observing light from a star now can actually change
   what happened in the past, when the light was first emitted. If there is
   any truth to that, try wrapping your head around that one!

Take a cat and place it in a box alongside a bottle of poison that is broken if a Geiger counter detects the decay of a single radioactive particle. The vial might break, and it might not. It all depends on the detection of a decaying particle, and there is no way of knowing if the vial has been shattered and the cat has been killed . . . until the moment you open the box. Before the big reveal, the cat has two possible states of existence—alive or dead—and there is no knowing which is true. In effect, before you peek, the cat is both alive *and* dead. But open the box and the cat's fate has been determined, because the act of observation has made one of the possibilities a reality.

That kind of thinking seems silly to those of us living up here in the larger real world, but Schroedinger is merely trying to help us understand what's happening in the subatomic world around us: very tiny particles appear to be able to exist in multiple states at once—until they are observed and measured. This ability to exist in multiple states at the same time is called *superimposition*.

The conclusion? At the smallest level of existence it is impossible to know anything for sure. What implications does that have for life in the bigger world? We really don't know yet.

The idea of an uncertain universe bothered to no end Albert Einstein, who came from a world of certain and pre-dictable outcomes. But in the brave new world of quantum mechanics, scientists could only predict *probabilities*. Writing in December 1926, he famously said, "Quantum theory yields much, but it hardly brings us close to the Old One's secrets. I, in any case, am convinced He does not play dice with the universe."[3] The Old One, of course, is God—although Einstein did not actually believe in a *personal* God.

---

3   https://www.stmarys.ac.uk/news/2014/09/physics-beyond-god-play-dice-
     einstein-mean/

The great Einstein, in other words, could not wrap his head around an entirely unpredictable physical universe. He is also credited with saying, "The more I learn, the more I realize how much I don't know."

He could be speaking for all of us. Finding certainty—and predicting the future—appears to be less possible than our ancestors believed. History would appear to be a chain of random events that nobody could have anticipated. Things just *happen*, without rhyme or reason.

That would mean, of course, that everything around us just happened. The rise of American global dominance *just happened*. If you could go back and tweak just a few historical events, today's most dominant nation could have just as easily been found in some other part of the globe.

That is what makes the story of the Bible even more remarkable than we could have imagined. Somehow the Hebrew prophets managed to predict the trajectory of world history centuries in advance, in *stunning* detail. Prophetic celebrities such as Daniel and John were even able to *name* empires before they happened. It is a feat no human being could hope to accomplish; it points to a much higher intelligence involved in the creation of the Scriptures.

"Remember the former things of old," God says in Isaiah 46, "for I am God, and there is no other; I am God, and there is none like Me, declaring the end from the beginning, and from ancient times things that are not yet done, saying 'My counsel shall stand, and I will do all My pleasure'" (Isaiah 46:9,10).[4]

---

4   All Bible texts are from the *New King James Version*. Copyright © 1979, 1980, 1982 by Thomas Nelson, Inc. Used by permission. All rights reserved.

It is an impressive claim. Nobody *we* know can predict the future with any certainty. In light of the uncertainty at play in the universe, the claim is even more impressive: only the Mind that set the universe in motion could possibly see the end from the beginning.

So perhaps the appearance of the wealthiest, most powerful nation in the history of the world is not an accident at all. Maybe Somebody intended for it to happen, and revealed the rise of America to ancient prophets.

Let's travel back in time and pick up a handful of historical threads to see just how *non*-random the birth of the United States might be.

Chapter One

The country of Turkey forms a somewhat fuzzy cultural border between Asia and Europe. It is a place where East truly meets West. On some days and in some neighborhoods you will feel as if you are visiting Europe; on other days and in other places, the Middle East.

Back in the day when it was called Asia Minor, a name bestowed on the region by the Greeks,[5] it was on its way to becoming a flourishing center of Christianity. Four of Paul's pastoral letters are addressed to Christian communities in this territory: Galatians, Ephesians, Philippians, and Colossians. The apostle John served as pastor in the church of Ephesus, and his book of Revelation sends messages to seven churches located on the western edge of the region: Ephesus, Smyrna, Pergamos, Sardis, Thyatira, Philadelphia, and Laodicea.

By the fourth century the city of Byzantium in Asia Minor had become *the* major center of Christian influence in the East, after its name was changed to Constantinople in honor of the Roman emperor Constantine, the man who brought official state persecution of Christians to an end with the Edict of Milan. Today, however, it is no longer predominantly Christian; nearly 98 percent of the Turkish population claims to be Muslim.

---

5   The Greeks originally called the region *Asia,* but then expanded that term to cover a much larger portion of the Middle East. Most of what is now Turkey then became *Mikra Asia,* or Asia Minor.

It is not hard to identify the precise moment the shift from Christianity to Islam took place: April 1453. That's when Mehmet the Conqueror pulled up outside the formidable Theodosian walls of Constantinople with a massive super gun he had acquired from a Hungarian cannon maker named Orban. The weapon was an astonishing 27 feet long, with a bore large enough for a man to crawl inside. It also happened to be large enough to launch a 1,500-pound projectile for a mile.

There was sad irony in the fact that Mehmet owned such a formidable weapon. Orban had first offered to build it for the Byzantine emperor, Constantine XI, but the emperor could not even afford to build the foundry needed to cast it. He wanted the weapon, to be sure, so he tried to stall Orban and keep him in the city. Eventually, however, the Hungarian realized there would be no money anytime soon and left. He made his way to the Turks and offered to build it for them instead. Mehmet II, of course, was immediately interested, because the city of Constantinople had proven impenetrable to the onslaughts of many previous armies.

He had but one question for Orban: could it defeat the formidable Theodosian walls?

"I can cast a cannon of bronze with the capacity of the stone you want," Orban replied. "I have examined the walls of the city in great detail. I can shatter to dust not only these walls with the stones from my gun, but the very walls of Babylon itself."[6]

That was all Mehmet needed to hear, and he offered to pay more than the cannon maker was asking. Six weeks later the massive weapon was sitting outside the city of Constantinople,

---

6   https://www.historynet.com/the-guns-of-Constantinople.htm

ready to bring Christian power in the East to an end. The gun was so massive that it could be fired only once every three hours to prevent it from overheating. Mehmet also brought 80,000 Ottoman troops and another 69 smaller cannons, which could be used to continue a nonstop barrage on the city as they waited for the big gun to cool down.

On May 29, the battle was over, and a victorious Mehmet rode into the city. For three days, as was permitted by Muslim law, his men vandalized, pillaged, and raped. Eyewitnesses to the massacre describe the blood of Christians filling the cracks between the stones of the streets. Dead bodies clogged the waters of the Dardanelles, bobbing at the surface of the water by the thousands. Hagia Sophia, constructed by the Roman emperor Justinian as the largest Christian basilica in the world, was immediately converted into a mosque.[7]

The eastern half of the Roman Empire had outlived the West by nearly one thousand years. The West had already been shattered in AD 476, when its last emperor, Romulus Augustulus, was deposed by the barbarian commander Odoacer. Now the East was gone as well. It had been shrinking for years under Ottoman pressure, until Constantinople itself was just about the only portion of the empire left.

It had represented hope for Christians—a last holdout against the rise of Islam in the east. Now it was gone. Christians across Western Europe were in a state of shock. Constantinople had been the one prize the Muslims seemed incapable of winning. Where would they strike next? Would they be emboldened by such a victory? Would more of Europe now fall to their armies, as well?

---

7   It remained a mosque until 1935, when it was converted into a museum.

If only Rome had done more to help. It's not that Constantine XI didn't ask the bishop of Rome for help defending Christianity's eastern capital; he did. But he was informed that if Rome was to send reinforcements, the Eastern church would have to submit to the authority of the bishop of Rome and celebrate the Latin rite. The churches in the East were autonomous and celebrated the Greek rite. If they were to be rescued, that would have to change.

When desperation reached its peak, the church in Constantinople acquiesced to the demands of the pontiff and hastily held an ecumenical Latin service in Hagia Sophia. It was, understandably, poorly attended, and it failed to produce the desired result. Military help from the West never materialized apart from three Venetian merchant ships that brought some food and supplies. The Christians of Constantinople were left to fight the Turks alone.

Many Western Christians took the loss of Constantinople to be a sign of the times; Jerusalem had also fallen to Saladin's forces in 1187, so surely the end of all things was drawing nigh. There also were other indicators that the end times were approaching. The Great Famine of 1315–1317 had caused three consecutive years of crop failure, bringing about a famine so severe that it resulted in millions of deaths and reports of cannibalism. That crisis was quickly followed by the Black Plague, which killed anywhere from 75 to 200 million people, depending on which estimates you want to trust.

In 1377, the papacy, which had been headquartered in Avignon, France, for nearly seven decades, was returned to the city of Rome by Gregory XI. When the pope died the following year, Urban VI was elected. Those who did not care for Urban

VI, however, elected a rival pope, Clement VII, and established him back in Avignon. There were now *two* popes, a crisis that sharply divided the nations of Europe until the Council of Constance in 1414.

Many asked themselves: how could the papacy itself be torn in two unless the end was near?

Then Constantinople fell.

Among those hit hard by the news was a Genoese navigator named Christopher Columbus. He believed (as did many others) that Jerusalem would have to be liberated from the Muslims before Christ could return and judge the nations from His throne in the Holy City. The victory of Crusaders in Jerusalem in 1099 had been short-lived; the Muslims once again owned Jerusalem, and Europe was becoming increasingly fearful that she would never be able to turn back the tide of Islamic expansion.

Columbus knew that if they were going to displace the Muslims from the Holy City, they would need serious help. But where could such help be found?

Columbus came to believe that it might be found in the Grand Khan, king of the Mongols. Convinced that the end was at hand, a number of Franciscan missionaries had already made their way into the heart of Asia in the thirteenth century, believing that the gospel had to be preached to the ends of the earth before Christ could return. "And this gospel of the kingdom," Jesus had said, "will be preached in all the world as a witness to all the nations, and then the end will come."[8] The missionaries returned with a report that the Grand Khan had shown a passing interest in the Christian faith but struggled to believe that Christianity was an exclusive path to God.

---

8   Matthew 24:14.

A few years later a Venetian merchant named Marco Polo made the same journey after his father Nicolo and uncle Maffeo had been there to meet with the grandson of Genghis Khan. Through interaction with the Polo family, the Khan became deeply interested in all things Western, including the Christian faith:

Above all he questioned them about the Pope, the affairs of the Church, and the religious worship and doctrine of the Christians. Being well instructed and discreet men, they gave appropriate answers on all these points in the Tartar language, with which they were perfectly acquainted. The result was that the Great Khan, holding them in high esteem, frequently summoned them to talk with them.

When he had obtained all the information that the two brothers could give him, he was well satisfied. Having decided to use them as ambassadors to the Pope, he proposed to them, with many kind entreaties, that they should accompany one of his barons, named Kogatal, on a mission to the See of Rome.

His object, he told them, was to request his Holiness to send him a hundred men of learning, thoroughly acquainted with the principles of the Christian religion as well as with the seven arts. They were to be qualified to prove to the learned of his dominions by just and fair argument that the faith professed by Christians is superior to, and founded upon more evident truth than,

any other: that the gods of the Tartars and the idols
worshiped in their houses are only evil spirits, and that
they and the people of the East in general were under
an error in revering them as divinities. He said, more-
over, that he would be pleased if upon their return they
should bring with them from Jerusalem some of the holy
oil from the lamp which is kept burning over the Sepul-
cher of our Lord Jesus Christ, whom he professed to hold
in veneration and to consider the true God.[9]

What more proof did he need? Columbus had read Marco
Polo's book and knew of the Khan's interest in Christianity.[10]
If the Grand Khan could finally be converted, he could help
defeat the Muslims.[11] He was fabulously wealthy and powerful,
and exactly what Europe needed. If only *he* could approach the
Khan and convince him!

Of course, traveling to the Khan over land would be
impossible now that the Turks controlled Asia Minor. The only
other option was to sail down the coast of Africa, as Portuguese
and Spanish sailors were already doing, and sail around the
southern tip. It would be a long and expensive trip. *Too* long,
and *too* expensive.

---

9   Milton Rugoff, ed., *The Travels of Marco Polo* (New York: Signet Classics,
    1961), p. 38.

10 Columbus owned a Latin edition of Marco Polo's book, now housed in the
    Columbian library in Seville. There are at least seventy handwritten notes
    in the margins, indicating his great interest in the account.

11 The Mongols had already shown an ability to push back the Turks on their
    side of the Ottoman Empire. Mongol engagement with the Turks proved to
    be one of the factors that kept them from pushing further into Europe.

Was there another possibility? There was. He could sail *westward*, across the Atlantic.

This is the reason Columbus set sail across the Atlantic, quite contrary to what most of us were taught in school. He did *not* sail westward to prove to a backward and superstitious church that the world was a sphere. Anybody with a modicum of education already knew that. The Greeks had long before determined the earth was a globe—some 500 years before Christ, in fact. Then in 240 BC, a Greek mathematician by the name of Eratosthenes successfully measured the earth's circumference. His method was as simple as it was ingenious: he noticed that when he looked down a well in the city of Syene[12] at twelve noon on the summer solstice, his head would block the reflection of the sun in the water. That meant that the sun was directly overhead at that moment. Armed with that knowledge, he then put a stick in the ground at noon on the summer solstice in Alexandria, 5,000 stadia to the north. The stick cast a shadow, because the sun was now to the south instead of directly overhead, and the angle of the shadow was seven degrees, twelve minutes—one fiftieth of a circle. Eratosthenes then multiplied that 5,000 stadia by 50 and came up with a remarkably accurate approximation of the earth's circumference—within 100 miles of the truth, in fact.

The astronomer Posidonius made a similar calculation, using the position of the stars rather than sticks and shadows. His results were also incredibly accurate—but then were later revised by Ptolemy, who made an error and shrunk the circumference of the planet by several thousand miles. Columbus was

---

12 Modern-day Aswan.

likely in possession of Ptolemy's number, which means that even though he knew the earth was a sphere, that sphere was much larger than he believed. All of North and South America, in fact, lay hidden in Ptolemy's missing miles.

The idea *we* were taught in school—that the medieval church believed the earth to be flat? It's a myth. Perhaps unlettered peasants believed such things, but certainly not the scholars of the church. So how is it that we have come to believe that Columbus was trying to prove the earth round? It comes from a bit of creative license taken by the great American author Washington Irving. In his 1828 account of Columbus' life, which was at least partially fictionalized, he envisioned a panel of scholars at Salamanca questioning Columbus' sanity:

> *Columbus was assailed with citations from the Bible and the testament: the book of Genesis, the psalms of David, the Prophets, the epistles, and the gospels. To these were added the expositions of various saints and reverend commentators: St. Chrysostome and St. Augustine, St. Jerome and St. Gregory, St. Basil and St. Ambrose. . . . Doctrinal points were mixed up with philosophical discussions, and a mathematical demonstration was allowed no weight, if it appeared to clash with a text of scripture, or a commentary of one of the fathers.*[13]

He makes it sound as if Columbus was being questioned by the Inquisition, and that his heresy was the round earth. Irving's

---

13 Washington Irving, *History of the Life and Voyages of Christopher Columbus* (LEEAF.com Classics), Kindle locations 1441–1450, Kindle edition.

Columbus then defends himself against charges of ignorance and apostasy, to which a member of the panel mockingly replies:

> "Is there any one so foolish, as to believe that there are antipodes[14] with their feet opposite to ours; people who walk with their heels upward, and their heads hanging down? That there is a part of the world in which all things are topsy-turvy: where the trees grow with their branches downward, and where it rains, hails and snows upward? The idea of the roundness of the earth . . . was the cause of inventing this fable."[15]

It's an amusing story, but it never happened. Columbus' critics were well aware of the spherical world; their objections were based on the feasibility of such a long and arduous journey westward, a distance that was surely unrealistic. Some also questioned whether a ship could return from the West if it sailed up and over the edge of the globe, believing it to be impossible to sail back from the other side of a sphere.

The voyage of Columbus was not a scientific expedition; it was an effort to meet the Grand Khan, preach the gospel in the farthest reaches of the planet, and ultimately liberate Jerusalem so that Jesus could return. It was Bible prophecy that inspired Columbus, not astronomy or geography.

Columbus was convinced that his critics were wrong: crossing the sea between Asia and Europe *must* be possible, because he had already seen proof. In 1477, on his way back

---

14 Antipodes: a point on the opposite side of the globe.

15 Irving, 1459–1465.

from an expedition to Iceland (called *Thule* in his day), he stopped in the city of Galway, Ireland, where the locals had recently discovered two frozen bodies washed up on the beach. The deceased were clearly not European; to everybody's surprise, they looked Asian. In the margin of one of his favorite books, Pierre d'Ailly's *Imago mundi*, Columbus wrote:

> *Men of Cathay have come from the west. [Of this] we have seen many signs. And especially in Galway in Ireland, a man and a woman, of extraordinary appearance, have come to land on two tree trunks.*[16]

Cathay, of course, was the name Marco Polo had used for what we would today call *China*. It is exceptionally unlikely that the dead pair had actually drifted all the way from China, of course, but it is *not* unlikely that they could have been Inuit kayakers tragically blown off course, or North American Indians carried to the shores of Ireland by the Atlantic currents. Regardless of where they had come from, Columbus instinctively understood that they must have crossed the Atlantic. That meant that if *he* were to sail westward, he would not be trapped: there were currents that could transport him back home.

And if Jesus was to return, Columbus knew he *had* to make the crossing.

The conviction could not be shaken, and Columbus' interest in Bible prophecy began to deepen. He began poring over

---

16 Quoted in David B Quinn, "Columbus and the North: England, Iceland, and Ireland," *The William and Mary Quarterly,* vol. 49, no. 2, 1992, p. 284, http://www.jstor.org/stable/2947273.

the pages of the Bible in search of evidence that perhaps *he* had been commissioned by God to hasten the Second Coming. He also turned to the writings of a number of church fathers, and while perusing the writings of Augustine, he became convinced that world history had been divinely designed to last only a total of 7,000 years. In 1481, eleven years before his historic voyage, he ran calculations using the genealogies and chronologies of the Old Testament and came to the conclusion that the world was already 5,241 years old. That left another 1,759 years until Jesus would return, and he was relieved: perhaps the matter was not as pressing as he first believed.

Still, he couldn't shake his sense of urgency. Twenty years later, after he had already discovered the existence of the New World, he found himself dissatisfied with his original calculations, and, convinced that he must have made a mistake, he ran the numbers again. This time he came to the conclusion that there were only 155 years left—he had carried the gospel to the New World *just in time!*

Columbus was also attracted to the writings of a twelfth-century Italian theologian and mystic by the name of Joachim of Fiore, who dedicated himself to ferreting secret meanings out of the book of Revelation. Whoever would rebuild the temple in Jerusalem, Joachim said, would come from Spain.[17] Could it really be coincidence that his expedition had been commissioned by the Spanish monarchs Ferdinand and Isabella, and that he had brought them back incredible wealth from the New World—more than enough to finance the liberation of the Holy Land? Columbus thought not.

---

17   Roberto Rusconi, ed., *The Book of Prophecies Edited by Christopher Columbus* (Eugene, OR: Wipf and Stock Publishers, 1997), p. 77.

This Christopher Columbus, the Christian and student of Bible prophecy, is not the Columbus we heard about in school. Nor is he the ruthless monster that is now trotted out for negative news coverage every Columbus Day. The way the story is now told, Columbus was little more than a moral reprobate, so depraved that we question whether he ever deserved a day, a statue, or even a positive mention. Statues are being pulled down and paintings are being covered up in an effort to demote him from his formerly esteemed position in history.

There is some truth to the complaints about his character, to be sure. He proved to be a brutal governor, and his gubernatorial excesses cannot be excused. He was, in fact, sent back to the Old World in chains when his New World subjects complained about him. Columbus was also a product of his time: the church was just beginning to claw its way out of the Dark Ages, and Columbus was a part of that church. It would be a mistake to erase history because it is populated by people who did wrong things; soon we would have no history at all. (It is not hard to imagine that *our* descendants will be able to find what seem to be horrific chapters of our story—but they will be stories that seem perfectly normal to us.) To ignore Columbus the medieval Christian and Bible student is to miss a significant part of what actually happened.

It was a deep sense of prophetic destiny, not scientific inquiry or greed, that convinced Columbus that it was God's idea for him to cross the Atlantic. The evidence he found in the Bible and the writings of church fathers convinced him. He also found evidence in a handful of non-Christian sources, including a seemingly prophetic passage in a tragedy written by the first-century Roman philosopher Seneca:

> *There will come an age in the far-off years when Ocean*
> *shall unloose the bonds of things, when the whole broad*
> *earth shall be revealed, when Tethys[18] shall disclose new*
> *worlds and Thule not be the limit of the lands.[19]*

Thule is the ancient name for Iceland. When Columbus returned from his historic voyage, he was convinced that he had fulfilled the Roman poet's prediction: Iceland was no longer the most westerly land mass in the world, and now the church had become aware of the "whole broad earth." Columbus became fond of the passage and was convinced that ancient pagan seers were in agreement with what the Bible had predicted: Columbus had opened up the earth in answer to the call of God.

Most people are familiar with Columbus' voyage and his ships. What comes as a surprise to them is the fact that he also authored a considerable volume on the subject of Bible prophecy shortly after his third voyage—a collection of comments that were later compiled into a single book. The work includes a letter to Ferdinand and Isabella where Columbus describes the overwhelming impulse that compelled him to cross the sea:

> *During this time I have studied all kinds of texts: cos-*
> *mography, histories, chronicles, philosophy and other*
> *disciplines. Through these writings, the hand of Our*
> *Lord opened my mind to the possibility of sailing to the*

---

18   Or Tiphys, pilot for Jason and the Argonauts.

19   Seneca, *Medea & Thyestes* (LRP), pp. 19, 20, Kindle edition.

*Indies and gave me the will to attempt the voyage. With
this burning ambition, I came to your Highnesses. . . .
Who could doubt that this flash of understanding was
the work of the Holy Spirit, as well as my own? The Holy
Spirit illuminated his holy and sacred Scripture, encour-
aging me in a very strong and clear voice . . . urging me
to proceed. Continually, without ceasing a moment,
they insisted that I go on.*[20]

In another letter that he wrote to a friend of the queen,
Columbus said:

*God made me the messenger of the new heaven and the
new earth, of which He spoke in the Apocalypse of St.
John after having spoken of it by the mouth of Isaiah,
and he showed me where to find it.*[21]

His conviction that God had used him to hasten the return
of Christ was deep and unshakable. Even though he had failed
to reach the Grand Khan, he had still carried the gospel to a
distant group of people who had not yet heard it, and he had
also discovered a vast new source of wealth in the New World
that could help finance a final crusade against the Muslims
and liberate Jerusalem. He was wrong about the details, but he
was more right than he knew about the prophetic nature of his

---

20 *Prophecies,* p. 69.

21 Columbus to Doña Juana de la Torre, Raccolta di documenti e studio
    publications Della R. Commissioner Columbiana, part I, vol. II, *I Scriti di
    Cristoforo Colombo, ed. Cesar's de Lollis* (Rome: 1894), p. 66.

expedition. In ways he could not have possibly understood, he really *had* nudged the world much closer toward a final empire and the planet's prophetic endgame.

How? Buckle your seatbelt; the answer is likely to surprise you.

Chapter Two

YOU COULD DROP YOURSELF JUST ABOUT *ANYWHERE*
in history and pick up a thread that leads to the birth of
America, because there are thousands of them—enough to
defy the idea that the American republic simply appeared in
the eighteenth century as the product of millions of random
occurrences. It is far more reasonable to suggest that the United
States was the logical end result of philosophical thought that
steadily drove the world toward the revolutions that took place
on both sides of the Atlantic during the seventeenth through
twentieth centuries: the English, the French, the American, and
the Russian revolutions. These were the product of *ideas,* not
chance. In some cases those ideas failed abysmally, as in the
U.S.S.R., which did not manage to survive the twentieth century intact. They also failed in France, where the revolution of
the eighteenth century did not achieve the same kind of long-
term success and stability that the Americans realized.

The voyages of Columbus, we have discovered, were also
the product of ideas—distinctly Christian ideas. He was hardly
the first person to set foot in the Americas; after all, they were
already populated when he got there. In addition to the original
settlers, who apparently came from Asia, Viking explorers had
already established an ill-fated colony in Newfoundland five
centuries before Columbus. There is some evidence to suggest
that Chinese explorers had already made it to the west coast of

North America, and the distinct possibility that Irish explorers, such as Brendan the Navigator, made it to North America
almost a thousand years before Columbus.

The voyages of Columbus, however, proved to be
substantially different from all the others, because they
suddenly opened up the American continents to large-scale
European immigration. In other words, his discovery *stuck,*
and it was a game changer. You simply cannot understand
the rise of America without appealing to Columbus and his
prophetic convictions.

But there are other factors—more important factors—that
stretch back thousands of years before Columbus was born.
One of those is a story found in the Old Testament: the day that
Israel asked for a human king.

For the descendants of Abraham, asking for a monarch
was a radical move. Neighboring tribes had them, but Israel
did not—and for good reason. The children of Abraham were
a *theocracy,* ruled directly by God Himself. They had human
leadership, of course, in the form of judges and prophets, but
these individuals did not function like a king. They did not pass
decrees or draft legislation; they simply served as mediators
between God and His covenant people.

This was unlike anything found in the neighboring nations,
where monarchs often claimed that they did not merely *represent* the gods, but themselves possessed godlike powers. As a
result, their subjects often fell victim to the whims of inflated
egos and unbridled ambition and power. If a king was particularly selfish or corrupt, life would become unbearable.

As a result, we do not have the names of very many well-
loved and beneficent kings.

Israel, on the other hand, had a much better situation: they had a benevolent God who was deeply concerned about their prosperity and well-being. As long as they remained faithful to Him, living within the parameters of a voluntary covenant, no lasting harm could befall the Hebrew nation. Families and households became the focal point of the nation, with each household carrying the primary responsibility for a relationship with the Creator.

This winning formula, however, was radically altered the day the elders of Israel requested a meeting with Samuel the prophet:

> *Now it came to pass when Samuel was old that he made his sons judges over Israel. The name of his firstborn was Joel, and the name of his second, Abijah; they were judges in Beersheba. But his sons did not walk in his ways; they turned aside after dishonest gain, took bribes, and perverted justice. Then all the elders of Israel gathered together and came to Samuel at Ramah, and said to him, "Look, you are old, and your sons do not walk in your ways. Now make us a king to judge us like all the nations"* (1 Samuel 8:1–5).

Samuel's advancing age was a matter of deep concern for the Israelites. It would seem that they had perhaps elevated Samuel's prophetic office to a status higher than God had intended; they assumed that when Samuel died, they would be left without qualified leadership. This overlooked, of course, the fact that God Himself, not Samuel, had been guiding the nation. The prophet had been grooming his two sons to take his place, but Joel and Abijah had proven so corrupt that the people didn't want them, and rightfully so.

The elders panicked and took matters into their own hands. (One of the key lessons that is repeated many times over in the Bible is that people who try to assume God's place and take matters into their own hands usually create long-standing disasters.) They wanted a king like the neighboring tribes.

This story proves to be one of the biggest turning points in human history. God's intent had been to use Israel to demonstrate the superiority of His government to the surrounding nations. The sanctuary and its services were meant to foreshadow the coming Messiah and illustrate the plan of redemption. Through Israel, He planned to invite the whole world to join in the covenant of grace. "Even them I will bring to My holy mountain," God later told the prophet Isaiah, "and make them joyful in My house of prayer. Their burnt offerings and their sacrifices will be accepted on My altar; for My house shall be called a house of prayer for all nations."[22]

During the rebuilding of Jerusalem and the Temple after Babylonian captivity, God expressed the same sentiment to the prophet Zechariah:

> *Thus says the Lord of hosts: "Peoples shall yet come, inhabitants of many cities; the inhabitants of one city shall go to another, saying, 'Let us continue to go and pray before the Lord, and seek the Lord of hosts. I myself will go also.' Yes, many peoples and strong nations shall*

---

22 Isaiah 56:7. Jesus quoted this passage from Isaiah when driving the money
    changers out of the Temple, furious that His beacon of hope had been
    corrupted by human greed (Mark 11:17).

*come to seek the Lord of hosts in Jerusalem, and to
pray before the Lord." Thus says the Lord of hosts: "In
those days ten men from every language of the nations
shall grasp the sleeve of a Jewish man, saying, 'Let us
go with you, for we have heard that God is with you'"*
(Zechariah 8:20–23).

The problem God was trying to remedy through Israel was
significant: the human race had fallen from grace. We rejected
the order God established in Eden in favor of self-determination. City-states erupted across the face of the earth, each ruled
by human kings driven by selfish ambition. The first recorded
city in the biblical record was established by Cain, a man who
committed fratricide out of self-interest and jealousy.[23] Two
early cities that came to symbolize enmity against the government of God—Nineveh and Babel—were built by Nimrod, a
man whose selfish ambition and thirst for power earned him
the label of "mighty hunter before the Lord."[24]

Many read this description of the great Nimrod as a
compliment: what man *wouldn't* want to be a mighty hunter
before the Lord? This statement, however, is not meant as a
compliment; it is a description of prideful arrogance. Thomas
Whitelaw, in his contribution to the *Pulpit Commentary,* provides a fitting description of Nimrod:

*Though not one of the great ethnic heads, he is introduced
into the register of nations as the founder of imperialism.*

---

23 See Genesis 4:17.

24 Genesis 10:8–12.

Under him society passed from the patriarchal condition, in which each separate clan or tribe owns the sway of its natural head, into that (more abject or more civilised according as it is viewed) in which many different clans or tribes recognise the sway of one who is not their natural head, but has acquired his ascendancy and dominion by conquest. This is the principle of monarchism. Eastern tradition has painted Nimrod as a gigantic oppressor of the people's liberties and an impious rebel against the Divine authority. Josephus credits him with having instigated the building of the tower of Babel. He has been identified with the Orion of the Greeks.[25]

Human kingdoms were markedly different from the societal structure God intended for His people. Kingdoms were marked by ambition, arrogance, and oppression. One of Nimrod's key cities, Babel, would eventually become Babylon, the very antithesis of Jerusalem and the kingdom of God. Jerusalem was meant to be a contrast to worldly kingdoms, not a complement to them. In Jerusalem, He intended to demonstrate the foolishness of rejecting God and attempting to govern the world yourself. There was no need for a human king, and that was entirely the point: it was a precursor to the kingdom of Christ.

For God's people to request a king was to challenge God's entire purpose for Israel.

Troubled by the bold request, Samuel brought the matter to God, who expressed His disappointment and displeasure.

---

25   H. D. M. Spence-Jones et al., eds., *The Pulpit Commentary* (New York: Funk & Wagnalls Company, 1909), Genesis, p. 158.

But to Samuel's surprise, He instructed the prophet to give the Israelites precisely what they were asking for:

> *But the thing displeased Samuel when they said, "Give us a king to judge us." So Samuel prayed to the Lord. And the Lord said to Samuel, "Heed the voice of the people in all that they say to you; for they have not rejected you, but they have rejected Me, that I should not reign over them. According to all the works which they have done since the day that I brought them up out of Egypt, even to this day—with which they have forsaken Me and served other gods—so they are doing to you also. Now therefore, heed their voice. However, you shall solemnly forewarn them, and show them the behavior of the king who will reign over them"* (1 Samuel 8:6–9).

Unlike human kingdoms, the government of God is not built on coercion. If Israel did not wish to remain in the covenant, He was not going to force them to stay. This has always been the case: God has always allowed human beings freedom of conscience, including the freedom to choose against Him. Right from the beginning, Adam and Eve were free to turn against God.

Why would God take such a chance? God is defined in the Bible as the embodiment and epitome of love,[26] but there can be no such thing as genuine love if nobody has a choice. If we are to love God freely, there must the option of *not* loving Him or our choice becomes meaningless.

---

26 "And we have known and believed the love that God has for us. God is love, and he who abides in love abides in God, and God in him" (1 John 4:16).

But while God allows us to blaze our own trail, He does not do so without a warning; out of love for us, He shows us what will happen if we choose the wrong path. In Eden, the consequence for separating ourselves from God would be death—because to separate yourself from the Creator is to separate yourself from the only Source of life in the universe. When Israel requested a king, God did the same thing: He allowed them to do it, but not without a warning:

> So Samuel told all the words of the Lord to the people who asked him for a king. And he said, "This will be the behavior of the king who will reign over you: He will take your sons and appoint them for his own chariots and to be his horsemen, and some will run before his chariots. He will appoint captains over his thousands and captains over his fifties, will set some to plow his ground and reap his harvest, and some to make his weapons of war and equipment for his chariots. He will take your daughters to be perfumers, cooks, and bakers. And he will take the best of your fields, your vineyards, and your olive groves, and give them to his servants. He will take a tenth of your grain and your vintage, and give it to his officers and servants. And he will take your male servants, your female servants, your finest young men, and your donkeys, and put them to his work. He will take a tenth of your sheep. And you will be his servants. And you will cry out in that day because of your king whom you have chosen for yourselves, and the Lord will not hear you in that day." Nevertheless the people refused to obey the voice

of Samuel; and they said, "No, but we will have a king over us" (1 Samuel 8:10–19).

This divine warning, preserved by inspiration for the benefit of future generations, would prove to be an important incubator for ideas that would, thousands of years later, give rise to the American republic—a nation that was firmly established on the utter rejection of monarchy. How this is so will become apparent later on.

Duly warned, the elders of Israel persisted, and God's warning proved right. The long succession of kings that followed their horrible decision led the nation from one disaster to the next. Life was never again as good as it had been under God's direct government.

The affinity of Saul, Israel's first king, for God was short-lived; he quickly became like the kings of the surrounding Canaanite nations, driven by the same impulses. He was driven by pride, jealousy, and ambition. His apostasy was so thorough that after the death of Samuel, there was no more prophetic communication from God. Like other kings, he was left to stumble about in the dark, uncertain of what the future might bring. If he was going to be self-sufficient, then God would give him what he was asking for: utter and *complete* self-sufficiency, and it was in this condition that Saul had to face a war with the Philistines. Without a prophet to rely on, Saul panicked and went to a spiritualist for advice—a practice strictly forbidden by God. The news he received was not good: he would die the following day.

The next king, David, was a dramatic improvement over Israel's first king. He is described as a "man after His [God's]

own heart,"[27] and his kingdom was so successful and storied
that God used it to foreshadow the coming Messianic kingdom
of Christ. But as favored as David was, a human monarch was
still one step removed from the order that God had intended
for Israel, and even the nation's most celebrated king eventually
brought trouble on God's people.

In a story that could easily be mistaken for the plot of a
daytime soap opera, David had one of his most loyal soldiers
killed in order to cover up the adulterous affair he had carried
on with the man's now-pregnant wife. In addition to this blatant
moral transgression, David also succumbed to the temptation
to believe that Israel's peace and prosperity relied on his own
intellectual and military prowess. He conducted a national cen-
sus, a move that denied God's divine protection of His people,
and it resulted in a plague on the whole nation.[28]

The list of increasingly worse moral failures that took place
at the hands of kings after David would fill a book similar in
size to the Old Testament. (In fact, a sizable portion of the
Old Testament *is* devoted to recording this story.) Solomon,
David's son and the wisest of all kings, was permitted to build
the Temple in Jerusalem—an obvious moment of triumph for
the nation—but then he married a thousand women (counting
both wives and concubines), which led to the import of foreign
polytheistic religions and Solomon's personal downfall:

> *But King Solomon loved many foreign women, as well*
> *as the daughter of Pharaoh: women of the Moabites,*

27 1 Samuel 13:14.

28 2 Samuel 24:15.

Ammonites, Edomites, Sidonians, and Hittites—from
the nations of whom the Lord had said to the children
of Israel, "You shall not intermarry with them, nor they
with you. Surely they will turn away your hearts after
their gods." Solomon clung to these in love. And he had
seven hundred wives, princesses, and three hundred
concubines; and his wives turned away his heart. For
it was so, when Solomon was old, that his wives turned
his heart after other gods; and his heart was not loyal to
the Lord his God, as was the heart of his father David
(1 Kings 11:1–4).

After that, things got only worse. The kingdom split over
the issue of heavy taxation when Rehoboam, Solomon's son,
came to the throne. (Confiscation of personal wealth, of course,
was one of the things God had warned would happen under
human monarchs.) Now, instead of there being a united people of God waiting for the arrival of the Messiah, ten of the
tribes suddenly pulled away into their own kingdom. The ten
northern tribes then produced one of the most wicked kings
of all time: Ahab, a monarch who married Jezebel, a Phoeni-
cian princess, who immediately established the worship of the
Canaanite god Baal:

And it came to pass, as though it had been a trivial thing
for him to walk in the sins of Jeroboam the son of Nebat,
that he took as wife Jezebel the daughter of Ethbaal, king
of the Sidonians; and he went and served Baal and wor-
shiped him. Then he set up an altar for Baal in the tem-
ple of Baal, which he had built in Samaria. And Ahab

*made a wooden image. Ahab did more to provoke the
Lord God of Israel to anger than all the kings of Israel
who were before him* (1 Kings 16:31–33).

Jezebel's wickedness and corrupt influence over the nation
was so devastating that her name has come to represent unbridled wickedness. In fact, her name is used in the book of Revelation to describe the apostasy of wayward Christians:

*"Nevertheless I have a few things against you, because
you allow that woman Jezebel, who calls herself a proph-
etess, to teach and seduce My servants to commit sexual
immorality and eat things sacrificed to idols. And I gave
her time to repent of her sexual immorality, and she did
not repent. Indeed I will cast her into a sickbed, and those
who commit adultery with her into great tribulation,
unless they repent of their deeds."* (Revelation 2:20–22).

The problem with human monarchs, of course, was not
isolated to the northern tribes; Judah also strayed from God's
purpose. The book of 2 Chronicles, which was the original
ending of the Old Testament,[29] finishes with a heartbreaking
record of wicked kings whose abandonment of Abraham's God
eventually resulted in the Babylonians being permitted to sack
the city of Jerusalem and destroy the Temple.

29 Modern versions of the Bible have rearranged the books of the Old
Testament so that Malachi comes last, but in the original order, as you still
find it in editions that come from Jewish publishers, 2 Chronicles is the
close of the narrative. The story ends with Nebuchadnezzar destroying the
Temple, followed by a brief mention of the conquest of Babylon by Cyrus
and the return of God's people to Jerusalem.

The razing of the Temple at the hands of Nebuchadnezzar's armies was the original "abomination of desolation," a term that has often been misunderstood and misused in modern books about prophecy. Many times, a last-day "abomination of desolation" is imagined as some mysterious last-day outsider who makes life hard for God's people by setting up a rival religion. In the Old Testament, however, the abominations were perpetrated on the inside, by God's own people. The sins of wicked kings and the people who followed them were the "abomination that causes desolation," as it is rendered in many English translations of the Bible.[30]

Centuries later, when Jesus predicted the destruction of the Second Temple at the hands of the Romans, He used the same expression;[31] and again, the context makes it clear that it was the sins of God's own people, not the sins of the Romans, that led to the desolation of the Temple:

> "Therefore, indeed, I send you prophets, wise men, and scribes: some of them you will kill and crucify, and some of them you will scourge in your synagogues and persecute from city to city, that on you may come all the righteous blood shed on the earth, from the blood of righteous Abel to the blood of Zechariah, son of Berechiah, whom you murdered between the temple and the altar. Assuredly, I say to you, all these things will come upon this generation. O Jerusalem, Jerusalem, the one who kills the prophets and stones those who are

---

30   Daniel 11:31; 12:11.

31   Matthew 24:15.

sent to her! How often I wanted to gather your children
together, as a hen gathers her chicks under her wings,
but you were not willing! See! Your house is left to you
desolate" (Matthew 23:34–38).

It was Israel's disastrous choice to chart her own course
under human monarchs that eventually led to this "abomination of desolation": a ruined Temple in the heart of a nation
that had stubbornly refused the terms of a covenant with God.
It was a covenant that they had entered into voluntarily, and
abandoning it left them without God's divine protection:

Thus says the Lord, the God of Israel: "Go and speak to
Zedekiah king of Judah and tell him, 'Thus says the Lord:
"Behold, I will give this city into the hand of the king of
Babylon, and he shall burn it with fire. And you shall not
escape from his hand, but shall surely be taken and deliv-
ered into his hand; your eyes shall see the eyes of the king
of Babylon, he shall speak with you face to face, and you
shall go to Babylon"'" (Jeremiah 34:2, 3).

Because a God of love does not coerce relationships, His
people were permitted to have a king and then remain on the
path of apostasy. Ultimately, they received more than they had
bargained for: they were returned to the land of Chaldea—to
Babylon—the land their father Abraham had departed many
centuries previous.

It was as if God had returned His Son's unfaithful bride to
her ancestral home. They had requested a human kingdom, and
now they had one.

From that point forward the chosen people would never again enjoy the same kind of full political autonomy they enjoyed when God was their only King. Upon returning from Babylon, they were ever after subject to the power and authority of a Gentile nation (apart from a *very* brief and partial respite under the Hasmonean dynasty), and will remain so until the moment when Christ Himself comes to utterly overturn all our bad decisions and restore His rightful kingdom.

The tragic history of human kings and Israel is one of the important keys that unlocks much of the meaning of the Bible's key prophetic passages. But it is also the beginning of a long historical path that leads to the foundation of America.

Chapter Three

IN THE ANCIENT WORLD A VIVID, TROUBLING DREAM was not easily dismissed with a laugh, especially if you happened to be in a position of power. Perhaps the gods were trying to communicate something important, and if that were the case, you would ignore it to your own peril. So when the Babylonian king Nebuchadnezzar was suddenly wakened by a deeply disturbing dream, he immediately sent for his top advisors: the Chaldeans. Experts in fields that ranged from astronomy and mathematics to astrology and divination, the Chaldeans were considered the wisest men in the empire and served as the king's top advisors.

Dream interpretation was one of their specialties. When the king explained that his sleep had been disrupted by a troubling message from the gods, they asked him to relate the details so they could provide an interpretation and put the king's mind at ease. It was, no doubt, not the first time they had been called upon to perform such a task. But on this occasion, the king suspected that they were not genuinely capable of helping him:

> Then the Chaldeans spoke to the king in Aramaic, "O king, live forever! Tell your servants the dream, and we will give the interpretation." The king answered and said to the Chaldeans, "My decision is firm: if you do not make known the dream to me, and its interpretation,

*you shall be cut in pieces, and your houses shall be made
an ash heap. However, if you tell the dream and its
interpretation, you shall receive from me gifts, rewards,
and great honor. Therefore tell me the dream and its
interpretation"* (Daniel 2:4–6).

The Bible does not explicitly tell us *why* Nebuchadnezzar
suddenly distrusted his most prized advisors. Perhaps he suspected that *this* particular dream had not come through the
usual channels; that is, the Babylonian gods the Chaldeans professed to serve. The king's challenge, of course, was impossible:
there was no way they could reach into his mind and extract the
details of the dream any more than you or I could do it.[32] The
king was understandably furious; he had trusted his empire to
the advice of these men who now found themselves powerless
in the face of a dream that, unknown to anyone in the room,
had come from the God of the Hebrews.

Ancient civilizations thought of various gods as national
and territorial divinities. The Babylonians had their gods, the
Egyptians had theirs, and so on. But the God of the Hebrews
did not profess to be a regional divinity. He claimed to be the
God of the whole earth:

*"For your Maker is your husband, the Lord of hosts is
His name; and your Redeemer is the Holy One of Israel;
He is called the God of the whole earth"* (Isaiah 54:5).

---

32 To this day, we cannot truly read the human mind. We might use technol-
    ogy to guess what a person is thinking, or an MRI to see which parts of the
    brain light up when certain questions are posed, but nobody has ever been
    able to truly crack the secret of actual mind reading.

This, added to the fact that the Israelites were monotheists who rejected the polytheism of their neighbors, set the religion of Israel apart from the rest of the world. Abraham's God did not claim to be exclusive to one group of people or restricted to a narrow section of the planet; He claimed authority over everything and everybody. The dream He planted in Nebuchadnezzar's mind was meant to reveal that authority and put Nebuchadnezzar's kingdom in its proper perspective.

The servants of Marduk (and other Babylonian gods), of course, were incapable of discerning either the dream or its meaning, since it had not come from their gods. The task of interpreting it, much to the chagrin of the Chaldeans, fell to a young Hebrew named Daniel.[33] He asked the Babylonian potentate for time to petition his own God, which was granted to him, even after the king had lambasted his own trusted counselors when they stalled for time. A night of prayer, joined by three of his friends, unlocked the secrets of heaven, and the dream was revealed.

Daniel uttered a prayer of gratitude, which has been recorded for our benefit. The contents of his prayer highlight the key themes of the book that bears Daniel's name:

> *Then the secret was revealed to Daniel in a night vision.*
> *So Daniel blessed the God of heaven. Daniel answered*
> *and said: "Blessed be the name of God forever and*
> *ever, for wisdom and might are His. And He changes*
> *the times and the seasons; He removes kings and raises*
> *up kings; He gives wisdom to the wise and knowledge*

---

33   His name means "God is my judge."

to those who have understanding. He reveals deep and
secret things; He knows what is in the darkness, and
light dwells with Him. I thank You and praise You, O
God of my fathers; You have given me wisdom and
might, and have now made known to me what we
asked of You, for You have made known to us the king's
demand" (Daniel 2:19–23).

Here was the all-important point to Nebuchadnezzar's
dream: God has allowed the human race to go its own way,
build its own kingdoms, and live by its own principles. But even
so, He has not relinquished His claim on this planet. We may
have been granted freedom of choice, but God still has a hand
in steering world events toward the moment when *His* global
kingdom will be permanently reestablished. While it may
appear that kingdoms come and go because of random events,
behind the scenes the biggest movements on earth are being
choreographed by an Intelligence much greater than our own.

In other words, when an empire comes to power it happens
because God *allows* it.

That would suggest, of course, that when a nation as
wealthy, powerful, and influential as the American republic
emerges, it does not happen by chance, either. And sure enough,
the rest of this story provides us with important clues as to how
and why America was born. It bears looking at in some detail.

The symbol God used to reveal the political future to
Nebuchadnezzar was a statue made of various metals: a head
of gold, chest and arms of silver, belly and thighs of bronze,
legs of iron, and feet of iron and clay. This statue, Daniel
explained, portrayed a series of future kingdoms that would

rise and fall between the present moment and the end of the world. The head of gold represented Nebuchadnezzar and the Neo-Babylonian empire:

> *"You, O king, are a king of kings. For the God of heaven has given you a kingdom, power, strength, and glory; and wherever the children of men dwell, or the beasts of the field and the birds of the heaven, He has given them into your hand, and has made you ruler over them all— you are this head of gold"* (Daniel 2:37, 38).

That, of course, was good news; the God who had disturbed Nebuchadnezzar's sleep had favored him and allowed him to rise to the pinnacle of power. His kingdom truly *was* divinely appointed. Bad news, however, followed quickly:

> *"But after you shall arise another kingdom inferior to yours; then another, a third kingdom of bronze, which shall rule over all the earth. And the fourth kingdom shall be as strong as iron, inasmuch as iron breaks in pieces and shatters everything; and like iron that crushes, that kingdom will break in pieces and crush all the others"* (Daniel 2:39, 40).

These words were penned six centuries before Christ, and they have proven to be astonishingly accurate. Cyrus the Persian general captured the city of Babylon in 539 BC, establishing what was possibly the largest geographical empire in the world's history up to that point. The Persians, who allowed their subjects to retain their own culture and religion, allowed the Jews to return to Jerusalem to begin rebuilding the city and the Temple. This empire was represented by the chest and arms of silver.

The Persians were eventually displaced by the Greeks, who managed to conquer an unbelievable swath of territory stretching from the Mediterranean Basin to the subcontinent of India under Alexander the Great. Alexander's kingdom is represented by the belly and thighs of bronze.

The Greeks, in turn, were displaced by Rome, the empire that managed to sustain itself in one form or another for well over a millennium and a half—from its victory over the Greeks in 168 BC until the Ottoman Turks finally sacked the city of Constantinople in AD 1453. The Romans are represented by the legs of iron, a fitting description of an empire at least one notable historian has labeled "the iron monarchy."[34]

Should anyone doubt that these are the kingdoms intended by the dream, parallel prophecies found in other parts of Daniel clearly state it, even clearly *naming* some of them. Take, for example, this staggering prediction from chapter eight:

> *"The ram which you saw, having the two horns—they are the kings of Media and Persia. And the male goat is the kingdom of Greece. The large horn that is between its eyes is the first king"* (Daniel 8:20, 21).

---

34   See, for example, Edward Gibbon's clear use of Daniel 2 in his description of the rise of the Roman Empire: "The arms of the republic, sometimes vanquished in battle, always victorious in war, advanced with rapid steps to the Euphrates, the Danube, the Rhine, and the Ocean; and the images of gold, or silver, or brass, that might serve to represent the nations and their kings, were successively broken by the iron monarchy of Rome."—Edward Gibbon, *The History of the Decline and Fall of the Roman Empire* (New York: Kelmscott Society Publishers, 1845), vol. 3, p. 365.

You've got to wonder: how in the *world* is it possible that someone living six centuries before Christ was able to name Persia and Greece? And how was he able to correctly predict precisely four superpowers—not three, not five, but four?

It defies explanation, but there is still more to the dream. If someone were merely guessing at the future, you might expect a fifth and sixth empire to follow Rome—maybe even more. Or they might simply guess that the world would end after the fourth. But the king's dream reveals a detail that would be utterly impossible to know: the Roman Empire, it revealed, would break into pieces instead of being succeeded by another power. The iron influence of Rome would continue on throughout history, to be sure, but in a weakened, divided state, represented by the feet and toes of clay mixed with iron—and the fragments of Rome, Daniel predicted, would never be reunited nor return to their former glory:

> *"Whereas you saw the feet and toes, partly of potter's clay and partly of iron, the kingdom shall be divided; yet the strength of the iron shall be in it, just as you saw the iron mixed with ceramic clay. And as the toes of the feet were partly of iron and partly of clay, so the kingdom shall be partly strong and partly fragile. As you saw iron mixed with ceramic clay, they will mingle with the seed of men; but they will not adhere to one another, just as iron does not mix with clay"* (Daniel 2:41–43).

This is *exactly* what happened. Rome was not succeeded by another massive empire, but crumbled and became a mere shadow of her former glory. The first fracture took place as the empire divided into East and West, with Constantine moving his capital to Byzantium, a Greek colony located in Asia Minor. The city was renamed Constantinople in his honor and remained the capital of the Eastern Roman Empire until Constantine XI was deposed by Mehmet II in 1453.

The western half of the empire did not survive nearly as long, and it is here that the dream focuses its attention. The last Western emperor was deposed by Odoacer the Heruli king in AD 476. It then fragmented into much smaller barbarian kingdoms, which eventually gave rise to the nations of Western Europe. From that moment to the present, there has not been another Roman emperor in the West, in spite of the church's attempt to nominate various European monarchs as "Holy Roman Emperor," and the prediction that the shards of the shattered empire would "not adhere to one another" has proven stubbornly accurate. Every attempt to reconstruct a unified Western Empire, from Charlemagne and Charles V, to Louis XIV and Napoleon, to the Kaiser and Hitler, has failed emphatically and miserably.

Even the European Union, which is an economic rather than a political union, is having trouble keeping itself together.

The ruins of the Western Roman Empire, however, are still not the end of the dream. Before Nebuchadnezzar woke up, he saw a stone smash into the statue and destroy it. Then the stone grew in size until it overwhelmed and filled the whole planet.

It is not another *human* kingdom. It is the kingdom of God:

> *"And in the days of these kings the God of heaven will set up a kingdom which shall never be destroyed; and the kingdom shall not be left to other people; it shall*

break in pieces and consume all these kingdoms, and it shall stand forever" (Daniel 2:44).

The king's dream assures us that the present order of things, where we suffer under the inadequacy and corruption of human government, will not last forever. Our determination to govern ourselves has unfailingly compounded human suffering for many long centuries, but a God of love will not allow misery to continue forever. He has drawn a prophetic line in the sand, past which our experiment with self-determination will not be permitted to pass. And at that point, the kingdoms of this world will be permanently displaced so that His kingdom can be fully restored.

We are already living in the final moments of Nebuchadnezzar's dream—in the toes of iron and clay, which represent the monarchies of Western Europe. Somewhere, during that time, the world's greatest republic suddenly explodes onto the scene. That is *also* not a coincidence.

Chapter Four

It isn't easy being different. The chosen people were not at all like their neighbors, and they had been deliberately—*divinely*, in fact—established at the center of the ancient world, where the roads that connected Europe, Asia, and Africa met. Travelers who passed through the region would hear about the Creator that their own ancestors had set aside many generations before. The Temple and its sacrifices would illustrate the core problem with human existence and point to the only solution: the Lamb of God, Messiah.

Originally, the nation of Israel was a pure theocracy, with God as its only King; and even after the regrettable diversion to human monarchs, the Israelites were still substantially different enough from their neighbors that they came to view themselves as an island existing in a sea of Gentile nations. "The sea" or "waters" became a metaphor for the kingdoms that surrounded them:

> *Stretch out Your hand from above; rescue me and deliver me out of great waters, from the hand of foreigners* (Psalm 144:7).

> *Woe to the multitude of many people who make a noise like the roar of the seas, and to the rushing of nations that make a rushing like the rushing of mighty*

waters! The nations will rush like the rushing of many
waters; but God will rebuke them and they will flee far
away, and be chased like the chaff of the mountains
before the wind, like a rolling thing before the whirl-
wind (Isaiah 17:12, 13).

The establishment of a human monarch in Israel, of course, radically altered things to the point where God's people found themselves returned to Chaldea, the original home of their father Abraham. While in captivity—living *in* the sea, so to speak—a remarkable young prophet appeared in their midst who unveiled a stunning portrait of the future, detailing a long succession of Gentile kingdoms that would persist until the rightful King returned to displace human government with His own everlasting kingdom.

Decades after interpreting the Babylonian king's dream, Daniel himself received a vision while Nebuchadnezzar's grandson, Belshazzar, was serving as the empire's last regent. Instead of a statue, however, which was a symbol that would have spoken powerfully to a foreign king, Daniel saw the wind blowing on the Gentile sea, representing warfare and strife. As the wind blew, four animals crawled up on shore, one after the other:

In the first year of Belshazzar king of Babylon, Daniel
had a dream and visions of his head while on his bed.
Then he wrote down the dream, telling the main facts.
Daniel spoke, saying, "I saw in my vision by night, and
behold, the four winds of heaven were stirring up the
Great Sea. And four great beasts came up from the sea,
each different from the other" (Daniel 7:1–3).

The domination of Gentile powers over God's people would persist far into the future; Babylon would collapse, but she would be followed by others. The four animals that rose from the sea were the same four kingdoms outlined in Nebuchadnezzar's dream: Babylon, Persia, Greece, and Rome.[35]

Babylon:

> *"The first was like a lion, and had eagle's wings. I watched till its wings were plucked off; and it was lifted up from the earth and made to stand on two feet like a man, and a man's heart was given to it"* (Daniel 7:4).

When he saw this vision, Daniel was no longer a young man. Nebuchadnezzar had already passed from the scene. His grandson, Belshazzar, occupied the throne of the city while his father was busy elsewhere in the kingdom. The Neo-Babylonian Empire, about to recede into history, is represented by a lion with eagle's wings—a creature, incidentally, frequently found in the artwork of ancient Babylon.

Persia:

> *"And suddenly another beast, a second, like a bear. It was raised up on one side, and had three ribs in its mouth between its teeth. And they said thus to it: 'Arise, devour much flesh!'"* (Daniel 7:5).

---

35 The vision makes it evident that the animals, or "beasts," represent kingdoms. See Daniel 7:17.

In 539 BC, the armies of Cyrus the Persian toppled the Babylonian throne by diverting the Euphrates River away from Babylon and using the dry riverbed as a highway under the wall of the city. Belshazzar was hosting a drunken feast that night in an attempt to reassure its citizens that the city was unconquerable. Ironically, it was the feast itself that left the city unprepared for the sudden intrusion of the Persian hordes; none of the drunken revelers expected them to come *under* the wall, and the city fell easily. The father of history, Herodotus, recounts what took place:

> *Cyrus ... conducted the river by a channel into the lake, which was at that time a swamp, and so made the former course of the river passable by the sinking of the stream. When this had been done in such a manner, the Persians who had been posted for this very purpose entered by the bed of the river Euphrates into Babylon, the stream having sunk so far that it reached about to the middle of a man's thigh. Now if the Babylonians had had knowledge of it beforehand or had perceived that which was being done by Cyrus, they would have allowed the Persians to enter the city and then destroyed them miserably; for if they had closed all the gates that led to the river and mounted themselves upon the ramparts which were carried along the banks of the stream, they would have caught them as it were in a fish-wheal: but as it was, the Persians came upon them unexpectedly; and owing to the size of the city (so it is said by those who dwell there) after those about the extremities of the city had suffered capture, those Babylonians who dwelt in the middle did not know that they had been*

captured; but as they chanced to be holding a festival, they went on dancing and rejoicing during this time until they learnt the truth only too well.[36]

Daniel's vision portrays Cyrus and the Persians as a lop-sided bear ("raised up on one side") with three ribs in its mouth. Cyrus was a Persian; his grandfather, Astyages, was a Median king. Under Cyrus, the kingdoms of the Medes and the Persians were combined, with the Persians being the dominant partner in the coalition—thus a bear that was uneven on its feet. Cyrus took control of the three Babylonian provinces—Egypt, Lydia, and Babylon—which became three ribs in the bear's mouth.

Greece:

"After this I looked, and there was another, like a leop-ard, which had on its back four wings of a bird. The beast also had four heads, and dominion was given to it" (Daniel 7:6).

In 331 BC, the dominance of the Persians was brought to an end by Alexander the Great. While Babylon had a traditional set of eagle's wings, representing the speed with which she had dominated her neighbors,[37] the Greeks are portrayed as a leopard with a *double* set of wings. If Babylon was swift, Greece was swifter: in four short years, by the age of 32, Alexander had pushed the boundaries of his empire all the way to the Indian

---

36 Herodotus, *The Histories*, G. C. Macaulay, ed., vol. 1, book 1, sec. 191.

37 See, for example, Habakkuk 1:8, where eagle's wings are specifically used to describe the swiftness of the Chaldean armies.

subcontinent. The Jewish historical books of the Maccabees describe what happened succinctly:

> And it happened, after that Alexander son of Philip, the Macedonian, who came out of the land of Chettiim, had smitten Darius king of the Persians and Medes, that he reigned in his stead, the first over Greece, and made many wars, and won many strong holds, and slew the kings of the earth, and went through to the ends of the earth, and took spoils of many nations, insomuch that the earth was quiet before him; whereupon he was exalted, and his heart was lifted up. And he gathered a mighty strong host, and ruled over countries, and nations, and kings, who became tributaries unto him.[38]

In addition to four wings, this strange-looking leopard also has four heads, an uncanny prediction of Alexander's personal fall: on his way back from the East, Alexander suddenly died, and after a brief power struggle, his empire was eventually divided among four of his generals: Cassander, Lysimachus, Ptolemy, and Seleucus.[39]

---

38 1 Maccabees 1:1–4.

39 The book of 1 Maccabees indicates that Alexander may have made the decision to divide the empire himself, before he died: "And after these things he fell sick, and perceived that he should die. Wherefore he called his servants, such as were honourable, and had been brought up with him from his youth, and parted his kingdom among them, while he was yet alive" (1 Maccabees 1:5, 6).

Rome:

> *"After this I saw in the night visions, and behold, a
> fourth beast, dreadful and terrible, exceedingly strong.
> It had huge iron teeth; it was devouring, breaking in
> pieces, and trampling the residue with its feet. It was
> different from all the beasts that were before it, and it
> had ten horns"* (Daniel 7:7).

The Roman Empire appears different from the other kingdoms; it is not a recognizable animal, but rather a fearsome
beast with ten horns on its head. The ten horns represent the
divisions of the Western Empire after its collapse in AD 476,
just as the "feet and toes" of the image did in Nebuchadnezzar's
dream.[40] The horns are said to be "ten kings who shall arise
from this kingdom."[41]

Just as the iron influence of Rome persisted in the feet,
these ten horns are perched on Rome's head. In other words,
even though the Western Empire would collapse, Rome's
influence among the nations of Europe would persist until the
very end.

Further details about the same Gentile kingdoms appear
in both Daniel 8 and 11, and each time those details under-
score the fact that world history is not the product of random
events or chance. Somebody is guiding this planet to its grand
conclusion, when the rightful King takes back what was stolen
from Him. In Daniel 7, the conclusion to this parade of Gentile

---

40   Daniel 2:41.

41   Daniel 7:24.

powers is a powerful judgment scene where Christ, the Son of Man, is awarded His eternal inheritance:

> *"As for the rest of the beasts, they had their dominion taken away, yet their lives were prolonged for a season and a time. I was watching in the night visions, and behold, One like the Son of Man, coming with the clouds of heaven! He came to the Ancient of Days, and they brought Him near before Him. Then to Him was given dominion and glory and a kingdom, that all peoples, nations, and languages should serve Him. His dominion is an everlasting dominion, which shall not pass away, and His kingdom the one which shall not be destroyed"* (Daniel 7:12–14).

The vision is a complete sweep of human history, and it reveals *exactly* what to expect as we wait for this planet's ultimate redemption. But puzzlingly, what appears to be missing in Daniel's vision is the American republic. The power and the influence of the United States far exceeds that of any of the remaining horns, which represent the nations of Western Europe.

And there *is* an argument to be made that America is not located in the Mediterranean Basin, where it would qualify as part of the sea of Gentiles that surrounded Israel. (That would also explain why other great empires, such as those that appeared in China, are not mentioned.) Nor is it located in the ruins of the Western Roman Empire, which is the focus of Daniel's prophecy.

But still, given the timing of its appearance and its undeniable global influence, it seems odd that the prophecy would not include the United States. There is, however, a key detail in this prophecy that *does* start us down the path toward the birth of America:

> "*I was considering the horns, and there was another horn, a little one, coming up among them, before whom three of the first horns were plucked out by the roots. And there, in this horn, were eyes like the eyes of a man, and a mouth speaking pompous words*" (Daniel 7:8).

This is a new detail, one that was not revealed to Nebuchadnezzar. Among the ten divisions of the Western Roman Empire, an *eleventh* horn would appear—a horn that is markedly different from the others. This eleventh horn is described in ways that have, understandably, troubled Christian scholars for many centuries:

> "*Then I wished to know the truth about the fourth beast, which was different from all the others, exceedingly dreadful, with its teeth of iron and its nails of bronze, which devoured, broke in pieces, and trampled the residue with its feet; and the ten horns that were on its head, and the other horn which came up, before which three fell, namely, that horn which had eyes and a mouth which spoke pompous words, whose appearance was greater than his fellows. I was watching; and the same horn was making war against the saints, and prevailing against them, until the Ancient of Days came, and a judgment was made in favor of the saints of the Most High, and the time came for the saints to possess the kingdom*" (Daniel 7:19–22).

" 'The ten horns are ten kings who shall arise from this
kingdom. And another shall rise after them; he shall
be different from the first ones, and shall subdue three
kings. He shall speak pompous words against the Most
High, shall persecute the saints of the Most High, and
shall intend to change times and law. Then the saints
shall be given into his hand for a time and times and
half a time. But the court shall be seated, and they
shall take away his dominion, to consume and destroy
it forever' " (Daniel 7:24–26).

Daniel's little horn has long been identified by Christians
as an antichrist-type power, thanks to the mention of a persecution of the "saints of the Most High." And even though it
is a horn like the others, another kingdom, it is substantially
different from the others.

Modern books on Bible prophecy—particularly those published from the middle of the twentieth century onward—tend
to treat this "little horn" the same way they treat the "abomination of desolation," declaring it to be an outsider, someone who
establishes a claim to power along with a clearly false religion,
and who makes life miserable for God's people. That understanding, however, is distinctly modern. Our ancestors in the
church would have trouble recognizing it, because they understood something far more troubling by this "little horn" power
than an *outsider*. What *they* understood was that the biggest
problems outlined by the prophetic passages of the Bible have
almost always referred to God's own people. They are *internal*
rather than external problems.

When Jeremiah and other prophets predicted that the Babylonians would come to destroy Jerusalem, for example, it was apparent that it would happen because of the sins of God's own people. Jeremiah is known as the "weeping prophet" because of his heart-wrenching appeals to return to God. And the language he uses to illustrate Judah's unfaithfulness is not at all complimentary:

> *"They say, 'If a man divorces his wife, and she goes from him and becomes another man's, may he return to her again?' Would not that land be greatly polluted? But you have played the harlot with many lovers; yet return to Me," says the Lord. "Lift up your eyes to the desolate heights and see: where have you not lain with men? By the road you have sat for them like an Arabian in the wilderness; and you have polluted the land with your harlotries and your wickedness. Therefore the showers have been withheld, and there has been no latter rain. You have had a harlot's forehead; you refuse to be ashamed"* (Jeremiah 3:1–3).

Israel was supposed to be the covenant bride of the Creator, but she had been unfaithful, choosing instead to pursue the regional gods of her Gentile neighbors. The imagery is stark and deliberately shameful: God's bride has become a prostitute, giving to other gods what rightfully belongs to her Husband. The disturbing part of such language, which shows up repeatedly in the prophecies of the Old Testament, is its dramatic reoccurrence in the New Testament:

*Then one of the seven angels who had the seven bowls
came and talked with me, saying to me, "Come, I will
show you the judgment of the great harlot who sits on
many waters, with whom the kings of the earth committed fornication, and the inhabitants of the earth
were made drunk with the wine of her fornication." So
he carried me away in the Spirit into the wilderness.
And I saw a woman sitting on a scarlet beast which was
full of names of blasphemy, having seven heads and ten
horns. The woman was arrayed in purple and scarlet,
and adorned with gold and precious stones and pearls,
having in her hand a golden cup full of abominations
and the filthiness of her fornication. And on her fore-
head a name was written: MYSTERY, BABYLON THE
GREAT, THE MOTHER OF HARLOTS AND OF THE
ABOMINATIONS OF THE EARTH. I saw the woman,
drunk with the blood of the saints and with the blood
of the martyrs of Jesus. And when I saw her, I marveled
with great amazement* (Revelation 17:1–6).*

This should trouble us every bit as much as Nebuchadnezzar's dream troubled him. This unfaithful woman, clearly predicted for the New Testament era, is shown riding a beast with
seven heads and ten horns. That is precisely the same number
of heads and horns that rise out of the sea in Daniel's vision.[42]
Is it possible that the prophets foresaw the Christian church
repeating the same kinds of mistakes that Israel made? Is there
a tie between the woman on the beast and the little horn?

---

42 If you have trouble arriving at seven, remember that the leopard has
    four heads.

More disturbing: is the woman, in fact, one and the same as the little horn?

Add the thirteenth chapter of Revelation to the mix, and it certainly starts to look that way. Where Daniel saw four distinct animals coming out of the Gentile sea, John sees a single conglomerate animal made up of *all* the animals from Daniel's vision:

Then I stood on the sand of the sea. And I saw a beast rising up out of the sea, having seven heads and ten horns, and on his horns ten crowns, and on his heads a blasphemous name. Now the beast which I saw was like a leopard, his feet were like the feet of a bear, and his mouth like the mouth of a lion. The dragon gave him his power, his throne, and great authority. And I saw one of his heads as if it had been mortally wounded, and his deadly wound was healed. And all the world marveled and followed the beast. So they worshiped the dragon who gave authority to the beast; and they worshiped the beast, saying, "Who is like the beast? Who is able to make war with him?" And he was given a mouth speaking great things and blasphemies, and he was given authority to continue for forty-two months. Then he opened his mouth in blasphemy against God, to blaspheme His name, His tabernacle, and those who dwell in heaven. It was granted to him to make war with the saints and to overcome them. And authority was given him over every tribe, tongue, and nation. All who dwell on the

earth will worship him, whose names have not been
written in the Book of Life of the Lamb slain from the
foundation of the world (Revelation 13:1–8).

The eleventh horn—the little one that appeared in
Daniel's vision—grew out of the head of the Roman beast.
It was the ultimate product of the Roman system, which
persisted well into the life of Western Europe. It was the last
in a line of human kingdoms that stand in opposition to the
kingdom of Christ. In John's vision, it is made up of *all* the
dominant Gentile kingdoms, indicating that the beast he
saw is *also* the ultimate product of human kingdoms and
their resistance to God.

The ties between these three prophetic passages are unmistakable. The woman riding the beast "sits on many waters,"
indicating her connection to the world of Gentile empires, and
she commits "fornication," or spiritual unfaithfulness, with the
"kings of the earth." The conglomerate beast of Revelation 13
also rises out of the Gentile sea, and "all the world marveled
and followed" it. Both the little horn of Daniel 7 and the beast
of Revelation 13 are persecuting powers, making war with the
saints. Both speak "great words," or blasphemy.

And there is an impure woman riding the beast—a prostitute. That is God's prophetic description of His people when
they forsake Him.

What the little horn is describing is not a purely *politi-*
cal power. It is describing the church itself as it inherited the
political Roman Empire after its collapse, and it adopted the
abysmal behaviors it exhibited during the medieval period:
burning people at the stake, torturing people for matters of

conscience, and driving heretics from their homes. And maybe—just maybe—this little horn is the key to understanding the rise of America.

Chapter Five

TO REALLY UNDERSTAND HOW AMERICA WAS BORN, we need to pick up another important thread that begins some 1,700 years ago, during a time when the Roman Empire was in danger of becoming destabilized.[43] The emperor Diocletian, famous for his ruthless persecution of Christians, had decided to retire, and as he removed himself from power, a number of influential and powerful men made it their business to become his replacement. The massive empire was already being ruled by a *tetrarchy*, a carefully designed system where four men shared power: two in the East, and two in the West. But after the retirement of Diocletian, a fifth claimant to the throne emerged in the city of Rome, a man who felt he had been overlooked by Diocletian. His name was Maxentius.

Maxentius tried to usurp authority by convincing the Roman Senate to proclaim him emperor. It was an enticing proposition: the Senate was nowhere as influential as it once had been, and the act of choosing an emperor would reestablish its prestige. Constantine, the junior ruler, or *Caesar*, in the West (the senior ruler was titled *Augustus*), would have none of it and led his men to the gates of the Eternal City to displace the imposter.

---

43   I expound on the material in this chapter at some length in *Shadow Empire*.

In AD 312, Constantine defeated Maxentius at the Battle of Milvian Bridge, and because his mother was a convert to Christianity, he convinced himself that his mother's God had favored him. He quickly ended a decade-long formal persecution of Christians (one of the worst on record) that Diocletian had implemented. He returned the lands and churches that had been confiscated from Christians, and he began to favor the Christian faith—to the point where it became the official religion of the entire empire. Whether Constantine himself ever truly converted to Christianity is doubtful, but his victory and eventual political supremacy spelled good news for the followers of the Nazarene.

After a short stay in Rome, during which time he presented the Lateran Palace to the bishop of Rome as a gift, he pulled up stakes and moved to Byzantium, which was renamed Constantinople in his honor. The locus of power in the Roman Empire went eastward with him, and it would not be long before the glory days of the Western Empire drew to a close.

In AD 378, the Goths, recently arrived in Roman territory to escape the wrath of invading Huns, became angry about treatment they had received from the Romans and devastatingly sacked the city Adrianople. From there, with alarm bells ringing in the head of nearly every Roman citizen, they slowly made their way westward until they took the city of Rome itself in 410. By 476 it was all over: the last Western emperor had been deposed, and Western Rome collapsed in the face of barbarian pressure.

The collapse of the Western Empire left a devastating power vacuum in the West. Roman troops who were stationed in the far reaches of the empire started heading back home.

There were countless barbarian hordes who were more than happy to occupy the territories the Romans left: the British Isles were left to be overrun by Angles, Saxons, and Jutes, and the Celtic Gauls happily filled the vacancies left in France. Bit by bit the barbarian tribes that had brought Rome to her knees became the modern nations of Europe—and at the same time, they started converting to Christianity, essentially starting with Clovis, king of the Franks, in AD 508.

In the absence of Roman power, Christian churches began to fill the demand for governance, providing leadership and authority where the Romans previously had. Roman governors gave way to bishops, and the administrative structures once used by Rome were taken over by the church. We still see remnants of Roman administration in the structure of Western Christianity to this day: a regional administrative unit, for example, was known as a *diocese*, from the Greek word for "administration"; the legalized and liberated church after Constantine adopted this same term for their administrative units. Perhaps more tellingly, the title once assigned to the emperor, *Pontifex Maximus,* or "chief bridge builder," was now applied to the bishop of Rome.

It is hard to pin down exactly when and where all of the transformations in the church took place, but there is one important moment that is easy to identify. In AD 533, the Roman emperor Justinian, the man responsible for building Hagia Sophia in Constantinople, effectively handed the reins of power in the West *to* the bishop of Rome, essentially making him a new Caesar. He declared him to be "rector of all the holy churches," affirming him as the supreme authority in the church. And since the church was also now effectively the government, it made the bishop of Rome a Caesar in the West.[44] The church, under the pope's authority, became the new empire.

This marriage of church and state, however, was never Christ's intention. "You know that the rulers of the Gentiles lord it over them," Jesus told His disciples, "and those who are great exercise authority over them. Yet it shall not be so among you; but whoever desires to become great among you, let him be your servant."[45] God intended for the Christian church to be as Israel once had been: a place where people answered directly to God Himself, without a human ruler in between.

The rise of Constantine changed everything. In his earlier years, Constantine had accompanied Diocletian on some of his expeditions to eliminate undesirable sects from the empire, and he marveled at the courage and unbreakable unity exhibited by Christians. After his victory at Milvian Bridge and his subsequent consolidation of Roman power under himself, he viewed the unity of Christians as a kind of glue that could hold his newly unified empire together. If Christianity became the state religion, he believed, they would be as fiercely loyal to *him* as they had been to their crucified Master.

It wasn't long before the church disappointed Constantine with its apparent *dis*unity. A dispute arose in North Africa over the readmittance of *traditores,* or "traitors," to the church. During the Diocletian persecutions, a number of church leaders, instead of braving torture or death, fled the ranks of the church to save themselves. When the persecution ended, they wanted to be restored to their former posts, much to the chagrin

---

44 Historians sometimes refer to this development as *Caesaropapism*, where a bishop became an emperor.

45 Matthew 20:25, 26.

of those who had remained faithful. Some were so adamantly opposed to allowing their return that they even questioned the validity of baptisms they had performed in the past.

The church found itself unable to settle the dispute, and an appeal was made to the new emperor to assist them.[46] As a result, the bishop of Rome began to rise in prominence. Prior to this time, there had not been a supreme bishop; the Roman bishop had been one among equals, a leader in one of several major centers of Christian influence. But by association with the formal channels of imperial power, his star began to rise above the others.

On the heels of the Donatist controversy came a second squabble: a renegade priest by the name of Arius had raised questions about the full divinity of Christ, and again, the church seemed incapable of resolving the matter on its own. Constantine called together a church council in Nicea, a beautiful lakeside town in Asia Minor, where clergy from across the realm were assembled to settle the matter.

Again the influence of a temporal king was brought to the table, and *again,* the importance of the bishop of Rome rose.

Israel had asked for a king like their Gentile neighbors; the church had now invited the Roman emperor through its doors and assigned him authority that did not rightfully belong to him. Christians were now walking *precisely* the same path that Israel walked, and the church entered an era where political considerations began to hold at least equal weight with theological ones—and eventually, *more.* The kings of Israel had corrupted the nation with their own ambition, and now Roman-style politics were driving what was supposed to be the body of Christ in the same direction.

---

46   Again, this story is laid out more fully in *Shadow Empire.*

Power is irresistible to sinful human beings, and once political power became the norm in Western Christianity, the thirst for more control became insatiable. In the eighth century, a clever forgery known as the *Donation of Constantine* began circulating. It was said to be a decree from Constantine himself, granting ownership of the entire Western Empire's geographical territory to the church. It was a lie, of course, but it was believed long enough that the heads of European states found themselves with no choice but to bow to the wishes of the church—if they wished to hold on to their own power.

A woman, the Bible's symbol for the people of God, was indeed now riding the Gentile nations in a scandalous relationship never intended by Christ. An eleventh horn, a new kind of king, had emerged among the divisions of the former Western Empire. Daniel and John were precisely right: the Christian religion morphed from a humble, persecuted minority of Christ-followers into the most powerful political institution on the planet. And as Lord Acton so aptly put it, "power tends to corrupt, and absolute power corrupts absolutely."[47]

It may be painful to admit, but the medieval period—the Dark Ages, if you will—was not a shining moment for Christianity. The church behaved in ways never sanctioned by Christ, from rooting out heretics by force to burning them at the stake. In Spain, we forced Jews to either convert or lose everything. Some estimates place the number of those killed at the hands of the church throughout the centuries in the range of 50 million.[48]

---

47 The political power of the Roman bishop was the context for this famous quote from Acton.

48 Precise numbers, of course, are hard to ascertain. Some estimates were provided by people who were expressing anger at the Roman system, and should be treated as possibly polemical. One thing is not in doubt, however: countless people suffered at the hands of organized Christianity.

Jesus said, "Foxes have holes and birds of the air have nests, but the Son of Man has nowhere to lay His head" (Matthew 8:20), but the prelates of His church were now living like princes, buying and selling lofty positions in the church, and generating fabulous wealth from the gospel.

It wasn't difficult for thoughtful Christians to recognize that something had gone horribly wrong. From the earliest days of the political church there were voices decrying the abuses, and there were many appeals to return to a New Testament model. Then when calamities began to befall Europe, from the Black Plague to the fall of Constantinople at the hands of the Muslim Turks, many people started to suspect that Europe was under judgment—the way judgment had befallen Israel when *she* had strayed.

Both Israel and the church, people began to realize, had become spiritual prostitutes.

Then abrupt changes took place. The printing press was suddenly invented in 1440, and the first book it mass produced was the Bible. Columbus set sail to find aid for the reconquest of Jerusalem and discovered the existence of the Americas. And in Germany, an upstart young monk named Martin Luther started a continent-wide debate on the abuses of the church the day he nailed his 95 theses to the church door in Wittenberg.

Coincidence? Hardly.

The idea that the church had gone off the rails and that God had actually predicted it was like a bucket of cold water over the nations of Western Europe. Was it really possible that Christianity had gone bad? Were we as guilty as Israel, living in disobedience and disloyalty to God? From the vantage point of the twenty-first century, it seems obvious: of *course* we behaved badly; one need only point to the Inquisition to make the case. But to recently awakened medieval Christians, it was a tough pill to swallow. Countless scholars—including Joachim of Fiore (the man who inspired Columbus in his study of prophecy); Jan Hus, the preacher from Prague; Erasmus of Rotterdam; and the renegade monk Martin Luther—came to the same conclusion: God had predicted the apostasy of His church.

Bit by bit the lights started coming on all across the former Roman Empire. Christians suddenly found themselves with a lot of soul-searching to do, and, unfortunately, what should have been a discussion became a war. Catholic and Protestant princes went after each other in the Thirty Years' War (1618–1648), resulting in anywhere from 3 million to 11 million deaths. Protestants began to push back against persecution from Rome, but then, in turn, many Protestant groups started persecuting people who disagreed with *them*—such as the Anabaptists, who were anathematized for baptizing adults. (Many Anabaptists were punished for such "heinous" offenses against God by drowning, which was deemed an appropriate demise for those who wished to plunge people underwater.)

An unholy mess broke out in Europe—a mess that took centuries to create and started the day the church did what Israel had done: bring a human king into God's institution.

The Reformation of the sixteenth century was, of course, about a number of very important ideas. On the one hand, it was a call to discard the unfortunate thinking that had wormed its way into the church in the centuries since Constantine, and it was a call to return to the Bible as the church's supreme standard of faith. It was also a call, in the face of some very public abuses, to return to a simple faith in Christ as the only means to salvation. But at the same time, it was a deliberate attempt to free the Christian faith from a king that had been invited into the church.

Getting rid of the king, of course, was a very difficult thing to do. Even after we'd overturned the idea that political power over the nations should be invested in a single Christian bishop, we still had a difficult time letting go of power structures that had been in place for more than a millennium. The marriage of church and state was kept alive in a number of places—on a local level.

A good example of this can be found in the city of Geneva, a center for the Reformation teachings of John Calvin. In 1553, the city government, which was utterly blended with the authority of the local church, burned Michael Servetus at the stake for heresy. (Servetus had denied the divinity of Christ.) Ironically, those who put him to death were among those who had condemned Rome for using *its* political power to do the same thing.

Word of the brutal execution reached the ears of a former friend of Calvin's named Sebastian Castellio, and it moved him to start writing down some very important and seemingly radical ideas about religious liberty. He wrote under a pseudonym, of course, not wishing to suffer the same fate as Servetus, and his ideas began to take hold in the hearts of Christians who instinctively understood that the kingdom of God is not a *political* kingdom, and it is not built on force. Castellio's ideas—as well as the ideas of other proponents of religious liberty—started to take root just a few short years after Columbus discovered the New World. His thoughts, and the thoughts of others like him, became foundation stones for the eventual emergence of America, a place where the authorities of church and state would be strategically kept at arm's length from each other:

> *Such conduct [the persecution of heretics] is not actu-*
> *ated by Christ, as it seems to me, for He did not defend*
> *Himself by arms, though He might readily have done so,*
> *since He had at His disposal ten legions of angels. The*
> *oppressors are actuated rather by the desire to defend*
> *their power and worldly kingdom by the arms of the*
> *world. This appears from the fact that when they were*
> *poor and powerless, they detested persecutors, but now,*
> *having become strong, imitate them. Abandoning the*
> *arms of Christ they take the arms of the Pharisees, with-*
> *out which they would not be able to defend or retain*
> *their power. When I see how much blood has been shed*
> *since the creation of the world under the color of religion*
> *and how the just have always been slain before they*
> *were recognized, I fear lest the same thing happen in our*
> *day, that we kill as unjust those whom our descendants*
> *will revere as just.*[49]

"To kill a man," Castellio wrote, "is not to defend a doc-trine, but to kill a man. When the Genevans killed Servetus, they did not defend a doctrine; they killed a man."[50]

It was the rebirth of a *very* important idea—the idea that people with different belief systems might actually be able to

---

49 Roland Bainton, ed., *Concerning Heretics by Sebastian Castellio* (New York: Octagon Books, 1979), p. 226.

50 Ibid., p. 271.

coexist, particularly if the church did not wield political power. After more than a thousand years of church and state, it was a difficult idea for many people to process. If you didn't use *force* to keep people in line, what would you use?

The answer was reason. Persuasion.

The liberties that we enjoy in the modern Western world are a relatively new thing, born of ideas that came at a very high price as the people of Western Europe sorted through the difficult issue of what life would look like if the church was no longer running the state, and the state was no longer running the church. The reins of political power had been mostly wrenched from the bishop of Rome, but sorting out the aftermath would take time.

It was this struggle for the church, described in the New Testament, which led to one of the boldest ideas in the history of the world: a new republic where church and state would actually be formally separated by law.

To get from Castellio to America, however, we'll have to visit a small city in the Netherlands.

Chapter Six

IN 1649, A COURT ESTABLISHED BY OLIVER CROMWELL'S Rump Parliament did something never before done in England: they tried a king for treason. Nearly 85,000 people had died in two civil wars, and Charles I, they believed, must be held accountable for his crimes against the people. The charge:

> *All which wicked designs, wars, and evil practices of him, the said Charles Stuart, have been, and are carried on for the advancement and upholding of a personal interest of will, power, and pretended prerogative to himself and his family, against the public interest, common right, liberty, justice, and peace of the people of this nation, by and from whom he was entrusted as aforesaid. By all which it appeareth that the said Charles Stuart hath been, and is the occasioner, author, and continuer of the said unnatural, cruel and bloody wars; and therein guilty of all the treasons, murders, rapines, burnings, spoils, desolations, damages and mischiefs to this nation, acted and committed in the said wars, or occasioned thereby.*[51]

---

51 Samuel Rawson Gardiner, ed., "The Charge against the King," *The Constitutional Documents of the Puritan Revolution 1625–1660* (Oxford: Oxford University Press, 1906).

Essentially, the complaint against Charles was that he had used his office to pursue personal interests over the good of the people—a complaint that could have easily been lodged against nearly every monarch from every nation in every age. It falls right in line with God's warning to Israel: a king will serve himself instead of the people.

The court was stacked against the king; Oliver Cromwell handpicked 68 judges to try him. Charles, a firm believer in the divine right of kings[52] (like most of his regal ancestors), refused to accept that Cromwell's court had any legal or moral authority. He also appeared to doubt that the trial would lead to any real consequences. He remained defiant during the proceedings, demanding to know by what authority these men had dared put him on trial.

Charging a king with treason was ludicrous, he believed, because the very definition of treason was betrayal of the *king!*

Charles I insisted that he would answer to the charge of treason only if the court could prove they had the God-given right to try him. His assertion went unanswered; nobody attempted to prove that the court had authority—they simply proceeded as if they did.

Then suddenly a macabre bit of foreshadowing presented itself: the king, attempting to get the attention of a court official, reached out with his cane to poke him and the top of the cane fell off, landing noisily on the floor. Whereas someone else would have bent over to retrieve it, Charles remained still, waiting for an underling to come and pick it up for him.

---

52   The doctrine that kings are appointed by God and have a divine right to rule—that their authority derives from God and not through consent of the governed.

Kings simply do *not* retrieve things from the floor—that is what servants do!

Nobody moved, and that's when it finally dawned on Charles: he was not being tried as a *king*, but as a *man*. The decapitated cane bore witness to what was about to happen: on the twenty-fifth of January he was convicted and then sentenced to death by *beheading*.

The execution itself was a pedestrian affair. There was no pomp or ceremony added to the event to indicate that the man being executed was special. The king's head came off of his shoulders with a single blow, which suggested that the man who performed the grisly deed was experienced at beheadings. No special executioner had been summoned; rather, the king was put to death like a commoner. Moments after his head hit the ground, the executioner grabbed it, hoisted it high above the crowd, and shouted, "Behold the head of a traitor!"

A good bedtime story for children? No. But it *is* one of the most important moments in European history, and it provides another historical thread we must pick up and follow if we are to understand the birth of America. The common people had tried and executed a king, which meant that a new idea was taking root: the universal rule of law, where even a king must be subject to the same laws as his subjects.

It was a violent way to make the point, and in reality Oliver Cromwell was anything but a saint. During his tenure as Lord Protector, he sometimes acted like the tyrant his men claimed the king had been. On one occasion he summarily dismissed the entire Parliament because he disagreed with their opinion.

Few of the heroes on the road to political and religious liberty were saintly. But with the execution of the king, the point had been forcefully made: the tide was turning, and people were starting to question just about everything, rethinking a thousand years of post-Constantinian social organization. The most thoughtful—and most influential—of these people abandoned swords and spears as their weapons, turning instead to the power of the pen.

The Church of England proved to be a disappointment to those hoping for religious liberty. It was, of course, notoriously founded on the basis of Henry VIII's sticky personal problem: he needed an heir to the throne, but his wife had proven barren. He wanted an annulment so that he could pursue a more fertile mate, but the bishop of Rome refused to grant it. This was at a time when many of the German princes had already managed to shake off the pope's authority, however, so the idea of breaking away from Rome was already on the table in Western Europe. Henry decided that he, too, would walk out from under the Roman umbrella and become the head of a new, independent church. In 1531, he was declared the Supreme Head of the Church of England.

A new English church must have seemed hopeful to many people living in the British Isles: perhaps it meant that *they* could also exercise independence and find freedom of religious expression. But that is not at all what happened.

By the time the seventeenth century dawned, it was obvious that English Christians had exchanged one form of religious tyranny for another: the new Church of England was not merely a new religious option—it was compulsory. By 1593, there was a law known as the *Conventicle Act,* forbidding any religious gathering of more than five people outside of an officially sanctioned parish church. Running a home church could land you in jail. After Cromwell, when the English monarchy was restored in 1660, another law was passed: the *Act of Uniformity*, which mandated that all clergy must be ordained by the Anglican bishop, and all church services must be conducted according to the Book of Common Prayer.

There was no room for creativity, no room for varied divergent religious practice (at least not in public), and no room for difference of opinion, no matter how sincerely held. The promise of liberty had been an illusion.

For the English who wished to worship God according to the dictates of personal conscience, the seventeenth century was not a happy time. In some ways, with the new locus of power so much closer to home, the situation was worse than it had been under Rome. The number of dissenting religious groups affected by this new marriage of church and state was significant.

The Barrowists, for example, believed that individuals did not require the sanction of the state to worship God freely. The Fifth Monarchists (also Puritans) had studied the four kingdoms of Daniel's prophecies and decided (quite correctly) that the next global empire would not be another human kingdom, but the kingdom of Christ. The Levelers pushed for religious liberty and equal rights based on natural law and as expressed in the Bible. The Diggers, proto-anarchist radicals who considered the Levelers to be too mild, wished to practice an economic equality they believed was described in the book of Acts. The Puritans, while not opposed to a national church (if it was distinctly Calvinist), stressed individual responsibility in a personal relationship with God. Sabbatarians, upon discovering that the Sabbath had been changed from Saturday to Sunday centuries after Christ's ascension, and not by a command found in Scripture, wished to worship on the seventh day of the week. The Quakers wished to experience a personal relationship with Christ without the need to go through members of the clergy.

The list of dissenting religious groups that emerged in the seventeenth century is long. None of them were permitted to worship freely. Many of them were persecuted for trying.

This was a period during which a number of now well-known Christian thinkers and writers emerged, not the least of which was John Bunyan, author of the much-celebrated *Pilgrim's Progress*. The book was written in prison, where Bunyan was being punished for violating the Conventicle Act because he had been worshiping and preaching in private. In 1661, Bunyan was informed that if he agreed to stop preaching and return to the state-sanctioned church, he would serve only a three-month sentence. If he refused to comply, he would remain in prison. He remained locked up at Bedford County Gaol for twelve years.

Some people, such as Oliver Cromwell and his men, realizing that monarchical oppression was not likely to go away any time soon, took up arms in an attempt to change the nation by force. But others decided to emigrate and seek freedom elsewhere. Many fled to the Netherlands, which happened to be the freest republic of its day. The Dutch had somehow managed to create a society in which differing religious groups could live side by side without seeking to eliminate each other. It was one of the first successful experiments in European religious liberty, and if you lived during the seventeenth century and held divergent opinions, the Netherlands was the place to be. Many of the English nonconformists, or "Dissenters," as they came to be known, made new homes among the Dutch, joining other persecuted groups such as the Huguenots, who were fleeing France, and perhaps more important, Jews who were fleeing Spain to escape the Inquisition.

In important ways, Americans have the Netherlands to thank for the birth of their republic. The Dissenters who moved there were Protestants—people who believed that the best model for the Christian life is not found in canon law or long-held traditions, but rather in the teachings of Scripture. Most of the educated Dissenters could read Latin, the language of learning, but very few of them could read the Bible in its *original* languages: Hebrew, Aramaic, and Greek. But in the Netherlands they came into contact with a Jewish community that could teach them to read the Old Testament in Hebrew, and also provide them access to some very old Jewish commentaries.

That's when the story of Israel's request for a king suddenly passed across their radar, and they discovered that human kings were not God's original plan for His people. They wondered: could *this* be the reason they were still having so much trouble living under kings? Was it possible, if they had already thrown off the bishop of Rome, that they could *also* dispense with the monarchy?

This idea led to a heated debate, one of the biggest intellectual debates of the seventeenth century: what if it was possible to have a nation *without* a king? What if the "divine right of kings" was not entirely biblical?

It was clear to the Dissenters that God had been angry with Israel's request, informing Samuel that the request for a king was a rejection of Him.[53] God's people had been suffering under the thumb of oppression ever since. What would happen if they

_____

53   1 Samuel 8:7.

reversed Israel's bad decision? What if they could return to a social structure where individuals were directly and personally responsible to God, the way people had been prior to Saul's anointing?

In the 1600s, the idea of a republic without a king was revolutionary—sometimes literally—and the idea was irresistible. Before their blunder the ancient Israelites had lived in a republic rather than a monarchy. There was no king, and there was a supreme written law to which everybody was accountable—the Torah. A number of Dissenters actually began to describe the original situation in Israel as the "Hebrew republic."

It is a story that doesn't get much airplay today, where we tend to think of the Constitution of the United States as a product of the Enlightenment. And while the Enlightenment absolutely *did* play a role, the influence of Protestants armed with the story of Saul is a much more profound source. The impact is unmistakable.

As English Protestants began to explore the intriguing idea of a world without kings, they also dwelt frequently on the themes of Deuteronomy 17, where God predicted that Israel would one day ask for a king, and He established careful guidelines to mitigate the damage that such a poor decision would inevitably cause. The political guardrails mandated by God became key ideas that found their way into the establishment of American republicanism:

> *"When you come to the land which the Lord your God is giving you, and possess it and dwell in it, and say, 'I will set a king over me like all the nations that are around me,' you shall surely set a king over you whom the Lord your God chooses; one from among your brethren you shall set as king over you; you may not set a foreigner over you, who*

is not your brother. But he shall not multiply horses for himself, nor cause the people to return to Egypt to multiply horses, for the Lord has said to you, 'You shall not return that way again.' Neither shall he multiply wives for himself, lest his heart turn away; nor shall he greatly multiply silver and gold for himself. Also it shall be, when he sits on the throne of his kingdom, that he shall write for himself a copy of this law in a book, from the one before the priests, the Levites. And it shall be with him, and he shall read it all the days of his life, that he may learn to fear the Lord his God and be careful to observe all the words of this law and these statutes, that his heart may not be lifted above his brethren, that he may not turn aside from the commandment to the right hand or to the left, and that he may prolong his days in his kingdom, he and his children in the midst of Israel" (Deuteronomy 17:14–20).

The safeguards laid out in this passage seem ordinary to people living in twenty-first-century liberal democracies, but in the seventeenth century these were revolutionary ideas:

If there was to be a monarch, the king must be chosen according to God's guidelines. The top executive of the nation was not to be an autocrat, but personally answerable to God.

The king must not be a foreigner, but someone whose identity was wrapped up in the nation he was to govern. A foreigner might import ideas that would be detrimental to the covenant established between God and His people.

There was not to be a return to Egypt, even if it appeared to promise prosperity. In Egypt, God's people had been slaves, and in the new covenant nation of Israel, they were to be free. This freedom to live before God must never be compromised, and the people must never be enslaved. The king was not to grow wealthy on the proceeds of his office. In other words, there were checks and balances on his power.

Most importantly, the king would be subject to the rule of law, just like any other citizen. In reality, he was held to be *more* responsible for the upholding of the law because of his position: he was required to make a personal copy of the written law and live by it the rest of his life.

The well-being of the nation was tied to the king's willingness to abide by the law.

The king, it turns out, was supposed to be a human being just like everybody else, with no intrinsic privilege before God. While he may have been vested with power and privilege, in heaven's eyes he was *not* above the people he governed. This is not the way that monarchs had been reigning; they had been living as if they were God's special children with *unquestionable* power and privilege. Kings had not been exercising their office the way God had required, but had been living more like ancient pagan kings who insisted that whatever came from their mouths may as well have come from the mouths of gods.

A number of Dissenters came to the conclusion that very early on, as God organized His covenant people, He had *not* intended to establish a monarchy but a republic. This was not an entirely new idea; the English had already been flirting with it for centuries, ever since the signing of the Magna Carta in 1215. Speaking of the Magna Carta, in 1260 Henry de Bracton, often called the "father of English law," emphasized that the king was also subject to the law:

"The king himself ought not to be under man but under God, and under the Law, because the Law makes the king. Therefore let the king render back to the Law what the Law gives him, namely, dominion and power; for there is no king where will, and not Law, wields dominion."[54]

Intellectually speaking, for a very long time many scholars had already agreed that kings and governing bodies (such as Parliaments) must themselves be subject to the law. Practically speaking, however, this had not been the case in England. By the time American colonists were agitating for emancipation from the Crown, they were quick to point out that the rule of law was not in fact being practiced. Writing in 1763, on the virtual eve of the American Revolution, James Otis argued that neither king nor parliament was above "natural" law, or the law established by God Himself:

To say the parliament is absolute and arbitrary, is a contradiction. The parliament cannot make 2 and 2, 5; Omnipotency cannot do it. The supreme power in a state, is jus dicere only;—jus dare, strictly speaking, belongs alone to God. Parliaments are in all cases to declare what is parliament that makes it so: There must be in every instance, a higher authority, viz. GOD.

---

54 Quoted in James McClellan, *Liberty, Order, and Justice: An Introduction to the Constitutional Principles of American Government*, 3rd ed. (Indianapolis: Liberty Fund, 2000), Part 4. Basic Constitutional Concepts: Federalism, Separation of Powers, and the Rule of Law, section C. "The Rule of Law and The Basic Principles of the American Constitution," pp. 347–354.

Should an act of parliament be against any of his natural laws, which are immutably true, their declaration would be contrary to eternal truth, equity and justice, and consequently void: and so it would be adjudged by the parliament itself, when convinced of their mistake. Upon this great principle, parliaments repeal such acts, as soon as they find they have been mistaken, in having declared them to be for the public good, when in fact they were not so.[55]

The biblical ideas about governance being considered by the Dissenters in the seventeenth century appeared a century later in the wording of the American Constitution:

No Person except a natural born Citizen, or a Citizen of the United States, at the time of the Adoption of this Constitution, shall be eligible to the Office of President; neither shall any Person be eligible to that Office who shall not have attained to the Age of thirty five Years, and been fourteen Years a Resident within the United States. (Article II, Section 1, Clause 5)

The President shall, at stated Times, receive for his Services, a Compensation, which shall neither be increased nor diminished during the Period for which he shall have been elected, and he shall not receive within that Period any other Emolument from the United States, or any of them. (Article II, Section 1, Clause 7)

---

55   James Otis, *Rights of British Colonies Asserted*, 1763.

This Constitution, and the Laws of the United States which shall be made in Pursuance thereof; and all Treaties made, or which shall be made, under the Authority of the United States, shall be the supreme Law of the Land; and the Judges in every State shall be bound thereby, any Thing in the Constitution or Laws of any State to the Contrary notwithstanding. (Article VI, Clause 2)[56]

These concepts in the American Constitution were neither new nor accidental: they had been fomenting in the minds of Protestants for many years, and were built on long millennia of political and religious discourse before that. Among other things, the founders had been reading the writings of John Locke, who had been forced to hide in the Netherlands when he was accused of plotting to kill the English king. While in exile, Locke wrote *A Letter Concerning Toleration,* which made powerful arguments suggesting that the proper sphere of government should be restricted to *civil* matters, and that spiritual matters were the proper sphere of the church:

The only business of the church is the salvation of souls, and it no way concerns the commonwealth, or any member of it, that this or the other ceremony be there made use of. Neither the use nor the omission of any ceremonies in those religious assemblies does either advantage or prejudice the life, liberty, or estate of any man.[57]

---

56 There have been attempts to argue that this section declares that laws made by government are also the supreme law of the land, making the legislative body, in effect, a law unto itself. Legislative power, however, is limited to activities "in pursuance" of the Constitution.

57 John Locke, *A Letter Concerning Toleration,* ed. James Tully (Indianapolis: Hackett Publishing Co., 1983) p. 39.

They had also read the works of John Milton, the famous poet, who argued for the rule of law and the consent of the governed:

> *It follows, lastly, that since the king or magistrate holds*
> *his authority of the people, both originally and naturally*
> *for their good in the first place, and not his own, then*
> *may the people, as oft as they shall judge it for the best,*
> *either choose him or reject him, retain him or depose*
> *him, though no tyrant, merely by the liberty and right of*
> *free-born men to be governed as seems best.*[58]

Those who insist that America was founded as a Christian nation are quite correct: there is little doubt that it was founded on principles of just government described in the Scriptures. This is different from what some people now insist "Christian nation" means, suggesting instead that the role of government is to enforce Christian morality by law. The founders, however, understood a Christian republic to be free from religious coercion, a nation that diligently guards the individual's right to personally respond (or *not* respond) to God as he or she sees fit.

Some of these new ideas made their way to the Americas on board the *Mayflower,* the ship that carried English Puritans to the New World. The passengers were religious Dissenters who had been living in the city of Leiden, Netherlands, in order to escape religious persecution. Today, we call these religious refugees *Pilgrims,* a name that neatly captures the essence of

---

58 John Milton, *The Tenure of Kings and Magistrates,* in Stephen Orgel and
    Jonathan Goldberg, eds., *John Milton: The Major Works* (Oxford: Oxford
    University Press, 2008), p. 281.

who they were: deeply religious people who were looking for more godly circumstances. The Dutch republic had provided them with a great degree of religious liberty, but over time they became concerned that their children were losing their English heritage and becoming Dutch, and because the Netherlands was an important center of world commerce, they also worried that their children might be exposed to undesirable worldly influences. So they did what millions of others have done since: they decided they could find a fresh start in the New World.

What they *intended* to do was settle in a relatively established area near the mouth of the Hudson River, but unexpected winds blew them off course, and they ended up in Plymouth instead, an area that had already been somewhat developed by the Patuxet Indians. Before their arrival, the Patuxets had been mostly wiped out by a devastating plague, and the few remaining survivors had already left the region. What awaited the Pilgrims was an arable piece of land that had already been mostly cleared, and—more importantly—they found life-saving stores of corn buried in the ground, enough to help them survive their first brutal winter in the New World.

Was their unexpected diversion to Plymouth accidental? When viewed from the larger span of history that arches over the settlement of the Americas, the Plymouth landing begins to look like an act of God. The Pilgrims themselves, amazed at the string of seeming "coincidences" that brought them to the region, began to believe that God had chosen the site for them.

There were just too many serendipitous events for them to believe otherwise—like the day they met Squanto.

Squanto's real name was *Tisquantum,* but because the English found that hard to pronounce, they shortened it. Prior to meeting the Pilgrims, Squanto had been kidnapped—twice—by Englishmen who took him captive to Europe, where he was treated like chattel. In time, he was liberated by Spanish monks and made his way back to the New World, only to discover that his people had been wiped out by plague.

His life had been devastated by Europeans. But like Joseph in the Bible, who was sold into slavery and ended up delivering his people from famine, Squanto came out of his trials equipped to save the Pilgrims. Not only did he speak English, he also knew how to live on the land and taught the settlers to raise corn and harvest the riches of the river. He was also able to help them negotiate a 50-year peace with the Wampanoag tribe, without which survival in their new home would have proven impossibly difficult.

Because of Squanto's involuntary sojourn to Europe, and because of the time he spent in the company of the Spanish monks who liberated him from his captors, he had already been exposed to Christianity and had adopted it. His idea of the Christian faith, of course, had a distinctly Catholic flavor to it, since he had learned from monks. The Pilgrims were staunch Protestants and Calvinists, which, under other circumstances, would have likely presented a barrier to cooperation. But the Pilgrims had come from the Dutch republic, where new ideas about religious toleration were being successfully implemented and diverse religious groups had learned to coexist. And, of course, the need to survive has a way of overcoming all differences.

This does not mean that the Pilgrims and Puritans who made their way to the New World immediately got it right. Changes in long-held religious perspectives are usually slow to take root, and the Pilgrims unfortunately managed to import some Old World ideas to the New. The religious colonies established by New World Dissenters were far from utopian. As other Puritans made their way to the Americas, the Pilgrim colony at Plymouth was eventually overshadowed by the Massachusetts Bay Colony, which in many ways continued to employ the church-state union that had led to their own persecution in Europe. The Massachusetts Bay Colony was not established as a center of religious diversity and tolerance, but as a decidedly *Puritan* community that provided religious liberty only for fellow Puritans.

When other religious minorities began to appear in the colony—such as the Quakers, for instance—old patterns of religious persecution ironically began to surface. At first the Quakers were banished from the colony, and a fine was levied on ships' captains who dared to bring Quakers from England. Hostilities began to escalate,[59] and the governors of the colony started confiscating Quaker property, cutting off Quaker ears, or even boring holes in Quaker tongues to prevent them from speaking.[60]

Eventually, they even resorted to the death penalty, the most famous case being that of Mary Dyer.

Mary Dyer proved especially problematic to the Puritans, given that she herself was a Puritan who had started questioning key doctrines of the church. By 1637, she was publicly defending the hated heretic Anne Hutchinson, who had been challenging Puritan clergy since the previous year. Hutchinson insisted that the Puritans had a legalistic approach to the faith, focused more on works than grace. Worse, she had insisted that God was able to speak directly to individuals without aid

---

59 https://nvdatabase.swarthmore.edu/content/quakers-fight-religious-freedom-puritan-massachusetts-1656-1661

60 http://historyofmassachusetts.org/history-of-the-massachusetts-bay-colony/

from the clergy, and that direct revelation by the Holy Spirit was at least equal to (if not more valuable than) the authority of Scripture itself. This, of course, was an unacceptable heresy, especially in light of the high price many English Puritans had paid for defending the authority of Scripture. In 1637, Anne Hutchinson was banished from the colony.

In 1637, Mary Dyer gave birth to a stillborn child who was tragically deformed. This was deemed to be God's punishment for heresy, and in 1638, she and her husband were also evicted from the community. Along with her husband, William, she moved to Rhode Island, where Roger Williams had established a community founded on the ideals of religious liberty and coexistence. In 1652, she traveled to England where she became a Quaker after listening to the preaching of George Fox.[61] Then in 1657, she came back to Boston in order to protest laws banning Quakers.

She was arrested and evicted from the colony. In 1658, she returned to visit two Quakers who had been arrested, and was again banished. After coming back a third time, she was sentenced to death. Her husband, however, was a friend of the governor, so she was spared while two others were hanged. (She *was,* however, escorted to the scaffold and had the rope placed around her neck as a warning.) She departed for Rhode Island, but returned once more in 1660, where she was finally hanged for heresy on Boston Common at the end of May.

With centuries of theocratic thinking in the background, the promise of genuine religious liberty was slow to take hold in the New World. Religious persecution continued to plague the colonies, many of them wishing to establish government based on their own religious preferences. The early days of American

---

61 Her husband did not become a Quaker.

colonization are replete with stories where religious minorities were denied certain privileges, and religious practices were either encoded in law or forbidden by it.

In 1610, for example, the colony of Virginia passed a law requiring church attendance on Sundays:

> *Every man and woman shall repair in the morning to the divine service and sermons preached upon the Sabbath day, and in the afternoon to divine service, and catechising, upon pain for the first fault to lose their provision and the allowance for the whole week following; for the second, to lose the said allowance and also be whipt; and for the third to suffer death.*[62]

Sunday observance laws came to be known as "blue laws,"[63] and in one now infamous case, a sea captain who had been absent for three years kissed his wife on the Sabbath—and was punished with two hours in the public stocks.[64] Even George Washington, after the birth of the American republic, was pulled over on his way to church for violating Connecticut's law forbidding unnecessary travel on Sundays.[65]

It is easy for some people to lose heart when they realize that our predecessors were fallible human beings, because we

---

62 http://libertymagazine.org/article/sunday-laws-in-america

63 It is rumored that they were called "blue laws" because they were originally printed on blue paper. But that may be a legend; the word "blue" was also used to mock the rigidity of Puritan moral codes. See https://www.britannica.com/topic/blue-law.

64 http://libertymagazine.org/article/sunday-laws-in-america

65 Ibid. He was released when he promised to go no farther than the church he was attempting to reach.

have a tendency to write flawless hagiographies of the historical characters we admire. (Likewise, we tend to condemn and dismiss people we might not care for, never giving them credit for that which they got right.) The stories of those who fought for religious freedom do not involve black-and-white morality, and the identity of villains and heroes is not always immediately obvious. If we are attempting to discern the hand of God in human affairs, we must remember that He does not force the conscience, so we must examine the general trajectory of history, understanding that God's raw material is fallen human beings. Like every Christian before them, the colonists were anything but perfect, and yet the fact remains: by the time the American Constitution was drafted, religious freedom had been enshrined by people who had seen something more desirable than theocracies and monarchies in the pages of the Bible.

There are many noteworthy names along the trail to liberty. We can thank trailblazers such as Roger Williams, who founded the colony of Rhode Island, where the separation of church and state guaranteed that individuals could practice their faith according to the dictates of their consciences. Or William Penn, the devoted Quaker who had been imprisoned in the Tower of London for his beliefs, and then went on to found the colony of Pennsylvania, where residents were free to exercise faith—including a settlement at Ephrata that decided to observe the Sabbath on the seventh day of the week, Saturday, instead of Sunday.

Compared to the pace of change in the Old World, where paradigm shifts in religious thinking unfolded over long centuries and were always hindered by more complicated political considerations, the shift toward liberty in the New World took place at an astonishing pace. As Victor Hugo once stated, "There is nothing as powerful as an idea whose time has come." The push toward liberty was unstoppable.

To tell the story of America and omit the potent influence of the Protestant Reformation and the English Dissenters is to miss *most* of it. The ideas that led to an official separation of church and state and the notion of government by consent of the governed did not rise in opposition to Christianity, but *because* of it. Even a casual glance through the works of important influencers such as John Locke, John Bunyan, Thomas Hobbes, and John Milton will demonstrate that the foundational principles of personal liberty were discovered in the Scriptures.

Rejecting the notion that the church should exercise temporal power over civil society, John Locke said:

> But this being not a proper place to inquire into the marks of the true church, I will only mind those that contend so earnestly for the decrees of their own society, and that cry out continually, The church! the church! with as much noise, and perhaps upon the same principle, as the Ephesian silversmiths did for their Diana; this, I say, I desire to mind them of, that the Gospel frequently declares that the true disciples of Christ must suffer persecution; but that the church of Christ should persecute others, and force others by fire and sword to embrace her faith and doctrine, I could never yet find in any of the books of the New Testament.[66]

---

66 John Locke, *The Second Treatise of Government and A Letter Concerning Toleration* (Dover Publications), p. 122, Kindle edition.

Speaking of the liberality of Persian kings to the Jews who wished to return to Jerusalem to rebuild the Temple, John Bunyan wrote:

And if all kings would but give such liberty, namely, that God's people should be directed in their temple-building, and temple-worship, as they find it in the law of their God, without the addition of man's inventions; and if all kings did but lay the same penalty upon those of their pretended servants, that should hinder this work, which this brave king Artaxerxes laid upon his; how many of the enemies of the Jews, before this time, would have been hanged, banished, had their goods confiscated to the king, or their bodies shut up in prison! Which we desire not; we desire only that the letter of the king might be considered, and we left to do, as is there licensed and directed. And when we do the contrary, let us be punished by the law of God, as we are His servants, and by the law of the king, as we are his subjects, we shall never complain.[67]

In the mid-seventeenth century, the political philosopher Thomas Hobbes explained in his landmark work *Leviathan* that the nation of Israel had originally answered directly to God, without the need for an intermediary human potentate:

But there are many other places that clearly prove the same. As first (1 Sam. 8.7) when the Elder of Israel (grieved with the corruption of the Sons of Samuel)

---

[67] John Bunyan, *The Ruin of Antichrist* (Swengel, PA: Reiner Publications, 1970), p. 8.

demanded a King, Samuel displeased therewith, prayed unto the Lord; and the Lord answering said unto him, Hearken unto the voice of the People, for they have not rejected thee, but they have rejected me, that I should not reign over them. Out of which it is evident, that God himself was their King; and Samuel did not command the people, but only delivered to them that which God from time to time appointed him.[68]

John Milton, famous author of *Paradise Lost*, argued that kings ought to be subject to God just as their subjects were, and properly governed only by the consent of their subjects:

Thirdly, it follows that to say kings are accountable to none but God is the overturning of all law and government. For if they may refuse to give account, then all covenants made with them at coronation, all oaths are in vain and mere mockeries, all laws which they swear to keep made to no purpose; for if the king fear not God (as how many of them do not), we hold then our lives and estates by the tenure of his mere grace and mercy, as from a god, not a mortal magistrate—a position that none but court parasites or men besotted would maintain. . . .

It follows, lastly, that since the king or magistrate holds his authority of the people, both originally and naturally for their good in the first place, and not his own, then

68 Thomas Hobbes, *Leviathan* (Markham, Ontario: Penguin Books Canada, 1985), p. 446.

*may the people, as oft as they shall judge it for the best,
either choose him or reject him, retain him or depose
him, though no tyrant, merely by the liberty and right
of free-born men to be governed as seems to them the
best. This, though it cannot but stand with plain reason, shall be made good also by Scripture: Deut. 17:14:
"When thou art come into the land which the Lord thy
God giveth thee, and shalt say, I will set a king over me,
like as all the nations about me." These words confirm
us that the right of choosing, yea of changing their own
government is by the grant of God himself in the people.
And therefore when they desired a king, though then
under another form of government, and though their
changing displeased him, yet he that was himself their
king, and rejected by them, would not be a hindrance to
what they intended, further than by persuasion, but that
they might do therein as they saw good, 1 Sam. 8, only
he reserved to himself the nomination of who should
reign over them. Neither did that exempt the king, as
if he were to God only accountable, though by his espe-
cial command anointed. Therefore "David first made a
covenant with the elders of Israel, and so was by them
anointed king," 2 Sam. 5:3; 1 Chron. 11. And Jehoida the
priest, making Jehoash king, made a covenant between
him and the people, 2 Kings 11:17. Therefore when
Rehoboam, at his coming to the crown, rejected those
conditions which the Israelites brought him, here what
they answer him: "What portion have we in David, or
inheritance in the son of Jesse? See to thine own house,
David." And for the like conditions not performed, all*

Israel before that time deposed Samuel; not for his own default, but for the misgovernment of his sons.[69]

The founders of the American republic drew a lot of their inspiration from the Christian writers of the seventeenth century, who, in turn, had drawn *their* inspiration from the pages of the Bible. It is in this sense that America was born as a Christian nation: it was built on principles of liberty enumerated in the Christian Scriptures and as a challenge to the Christian church-state compromise that had held Europe in darkness for many long centuries. It was no longer assumed that any human being had a divinely appointed right to govern others, nor was it assumed the Christian church had been established by Christ as an earthly, temporal kingdom. Those ideas had been imported into Christianity from the pagan Roman Empire, particularly after its collapse; *now* it was understood that Jesus had never suggested such an arrangement.

In the words of Jesus Himself:

"The kings of the Gentiles exercise lordship over them, and those who exercise authority over them are called 'benefactors.' But not so among you; on the contrary, he who is greatest among you, let him be as the younger, and he who governs as he who serves. For who is greater, he who sits at the table, or he who serves? Is it not he who sits at the table? Yet I am among you as the One who serves" (Luke 22:25–27).

---

69   John Milton, *The Tenure of Kings and Magistrates,* in Orgel and Goldberg, *John Milton: The Major Works,* pp. 280, 281.

Even Thomas Paine, hardly a traditional practitioner of Christianity (he rejected most organized, traditional religion and once famously stated, "My own mind is my own church"),[70] emphasized that the monarchs of Europe were more derivative of pagan culture than the teachings of the Bible:

> In the early ages of the world, according to the scripture chronology, there were no kings; the consequence of which was there were no wars; it is the pride of kings which throw mankind into confusion. Holland without a king hath enjoyed more peace for this last century than any of the monarchial governments in Europe. Antiquity favors the same remark; for the quiet and rural lives of the first patriarchs hath a happy something in them, which vanishes away when we come to the history of Jewish royalty.

> Government by kings was first introduced into the world by the Heathens, from whom the children of Israel copied the custom. It was the most prosperous invention the Devil ever set on foot for the promotion of idolatry. The Heathens paid divine honors to their deceased kings, and the Christian world hath improved on the plan by doing the same to their living ones. How impious is the title of sacred majesty applied to a worm, who in the midst of his splendor is crumbling into dust![71]

---

70 Thomas Paine et al., *The Theological Works of Thomas Paine* (R. Carlile, 1824), p. 31.

71 Thomas Paine, *Common Sense (Annotated): The Origin and Design of Government* (Coventry House Publishing), p. 11, Kindle edition.

The Jewish and Christian Scriptures had never suggested human government as the answer to our worst problems; God's solution had been to offer the human race a return to His kingship in a voluntary covenant relationship. Likewise, Christ did not seize the reins of political power during His time on earth, even though as the second Person of the Godhead, it would have been well within His means to do so. When Pilate asked Him if He was the King of the Jews, He replied, "My kingdom is not of this world. If My kingdom were of this world, My servants would fight, so that I should not be delivered to the Jews; but now My kingdom is not from here."[72]

The English Dissenters, in the face of persecution, understood that the kingdom of God is established by love and persuasion, not through coercion. They knew that the religious wars of Europe were a hangover from the Roman Empire, not an implementation of the principles of Christ. And in the constructing of America, the founders enshrined the right of all to pursue—or *not* pursue—God however they wished.

It was such a radical development in the world of Western thought that it leaves students of the Bible wondering: if the ancient empires of the world—Babylon, Persia, Greece, and Rome—were specifically predicted in Bible prophecy, then what about the United States? Surely, such an impressive latter-day empire would also merit a place in the divine chronology.

And it *does*.

---

72   John 18:36.

Chapter Seven

THE END OF THE 1700S WAS A REMARKABLY tumultuous time on both sides of the Atlantic Ocean. Ideas that had been fomenting in the minds of disenfranchised and dissatisfied Europeans and American colonists started to bubble over into political action. The French, motivated more by the Enlightenment than the Reformation, were eager to form a republic with a written constitution. They launched a bloody revolution that ended with not just the rejection of the monarchy, but also the Christian faith itself. Members of the clergy were exiled by the tens of thousands, and many were put to death. Churches were seized and converted into Temples of Reason, including the famed Notre Dame in Paris. Women were dressed as pagan goddesses and paraded through the streets to symbolize that the Goddess of Reason had usurped the place of popes and priests.

The French Revolution was shocking in its brutality. When Marie-Lavoie of Savoy expressed her support for royalty and refused to support the revolution, she was thrown to a mob in the street that quite literally ripped her to pieces. When religious peasants in the northwest of the nation resisted the regime's policy of abolishing Christianity, 170,000 of them were systematically slaughtered. Robespierre used the terror of the guillotine to enforce the new order, beheading tens of thousands.

It was a godless revolution, underscored by gratuitous violence, with an ill-informed Jacobin instinct to simply dismantle *everything*, without due consideration of the consequences—and it ended very badly. But on the other side of the Atlantic, the American Revolution had taken place with a strikingly different flavor . . . and results.

The founders of the American republic felt very strongly that the birth of their nation had been guided by God Himself, and in hindsight it is easy to see why they might believe that. When you consider the long string of historical events that all had to fall into place in order for America to happen, it begins to look as if a divine Hand had been guiding the process for centuries.

If Jerusalem had not fallen to Saladin, Western Europe might not have been spurred into action to resist the expansion of Islam, and a sense of apocalyptic urgency might not have taken root. That sense was heightened when the last vestiges of the Christian Roman Empire in the East were demolished at the fall of Constantinople in 1453—an event that led Christopher Columbus to examine Bible prophecy. His prophetic contemplations then gave birth to an overwhelming sense that God was sending him westward, over the ocean, to enlist the help of the Grand Khan to liberate Jerusalem and hasten the return of Christ.

Then, at about the same time—just prior to Columbus, in the middle of the fifteenth century—Johann Gutenberg invented the printing press. This enabled the mass distribution of the Scriptures, which were being translated into the common languages of everyday people. This was thanks to the efforts of reformers such as John Wycliffe, who had translated the Vulgate into English back in 1382, and William Tyndale, who by 1526 had translated the entire New Testament into English.

The sudden wide availability of the Bible led to thousands studying the Scriptures for themselves, which gave birth to the English Dissenters, who discovered that the practices of the state church were out of harmony with the teachings of Christ. Some were compelled to leave England, moving to the Dutch republic, where they were much freer to practice their faith. While there, they came into contact with Jews who had fled the Inquisition. That contact, in turn, further broadened their ability to understand the Old Testament, which gave birth to a whole new realm of political thought. They realized that God had established an ideal form of government in Israel: a *republic* established on the rule of law.

Given the chance to establish themselves in the New World, a group of those Dissenters boarded the *Mayflower*, which was suddenly driven off course by a mysterious wind. They landed in a place where the Pilgrims would not be impeded by the colonial governments of the Old World, or unduly influenced by other settlers.

The chain of events seems too convenient to be mere coincidence. And when the Continental Army took up arms against the British in the 1770s, they managed to pull off an inconceivable feat: they inexplicably defeated the most disciplined, most feared military force in the world. Knowing that their victory was improbable, they instinctively understood that God must have enabled it. That was certainly the opinion of George Washington at his presidential inauguration on April 30, 1789. Looking back on everything that had happened in the years leading up to the birth of an improbable nation, he stated that nobody should discount the indispensable role God had played:

"No people can be bound to acknowledge and adore the Invisible Hand which conducts the affairs of men more than those of the United States. Every step by which they have advanced to the character of an independent nation seems to have been distinguished by some token of providential agency."[73]

In a letter to the Reverend Samuel Langdon, Washington also said:

"The man must be bad indeed who can look upon the events of the American Revolution without feeling the warmest gratitude towards the great Author of the Universe whose divine interposition was so frequently manifested in our behalf."[74]

Two years previous, at the Constitutional Convention of 1787, Benjamin Franklin expressed much the same sentiment when he marveled at the improbability of the nation:

"I have lived, Sir, a long time, and the longer I live, the more convincing proofs I see of this truth—that God governs in the affairs of men. And if a sparrow cannot fall to the ground without his notice, is it probable that an empire can rise without his aid?"[75]

---

73 Quoted in Michael Medved, *The American Miracle: Divine Providence in the Rise of the Republic* (New York: Crown Forum, 2016), p. 71.

74 Quoted in Peter Lillback, *George Washington's Sacred Fire* (Bryn Mawr, PA: Providence Forum Press, 2006), p. 37.

75 Quoted in Steven Waldman, *Founding Faith: How Our Founding Fathers Forged a Radical New Approach to Religious Liberty* (Random House Publishing Group), Kindle edition.

These were not flippant remarks made by men wishing to impress a religious audience; the list of "coincidences" that led to emancipation from Mother England had been impressive. Every time George Washington's Continental Army was cornered, doomed to failure in the face of the powerful British redcoats, it seems as if some act of Providence would suddenly turn the tide in their favor.

Consider, for example, what happened outside the city of Boston in March 1776. Both Washington and the British understood the strategic importance of Dorchester Heights, a prominence that provided a good view of the city and harbor.

The colonists had closed in on the city, and Washington had brought 59 cannons for a siege on the British. The puzzle he had to solve was how to bring the cannons to high ground without being detected. On the night of March 4, Brigadier General John Thomas, with 2,000 of his men, quietly marched to the top of Dorchester Heights under cover of darkness. They wrapped their wagon wheels in straw to muffle sound, enabling them to move the cannons and prefabricated fortifications to the tops of the hills undetected. By four o'clock in the morning, they had built a defensive position above the city of Boston.

When the British woke up the next morning, they were horrified to see Washington's men commanding the hills above them. As one soldier told a London newspaper:

> *"This morning at day break we discovered two redoubts on the hills of Dorchester Point, and two smaller works on their flanks. They were all raised during the night, with an expedition equal to that of the genie belonging to Aladdin's wonderful lamp. From these hills they*

command the whole town, so that we must drive from their post, or desert the place."[76]

The British had no choice but to react, and swiftly. General William Howe ordered 2,400 of his troops to retake the position when night fell, using the cover of darkness as Washington had. There was little question in anyone's mind that they could easily displace the Americans, who were, after all, mere colonists. Many of Washington's men would have feared the same; the redcoats were a force to be reckoned with.

But on the night of March 5, when Howe's plans were supposed to be executed, an unexpected and severe storm suddenly blew into the harbor. Describing the ferocity of the driving winds, one of Washington's men described it as a "hurricane." The storm was violent enough that it started pulling up ships' anchors in the harbor, and two British vessels were blown ashore, suddenly making it impossible to deliver Howe's troops to the American position by boat. Then freezing rain and sleet started to coat the hills with slick ice, making it impossible for anyone to ascend to Washington's fortifications.

This unexpected meteorological event gave the Continental Army all the time they needed to strengthen their position. By the next day, General Howe became convinced that any attempt to recapture Dorchester Heights would be foolish and futile.

One such event might be dismissed as a fortunate coincidence for the colonials. But such events were regular occurrences: time and time again, the weather would suddenly change or something unexpected would happen to hand an unlikely

---

76 Quoted in Medved, p. 50.

victory to a ragtag band of Patriots who, by all accounts, should
have lost. On one occasion, George Washington found it necessary to evacuate 9,000 of his men from Manhattan without the
British noticing, a difficult feat at best—until a mysterious deep
fog suddenly settled on the island, making his men invisible.

The sense that God had intervened repeatedly in behalf of
the colonists was so strong that mere days after the Declaration of Independence, Virginia statesman John Page wrote to
Thomas Jefferson:

> *"God preserve the United States. We know the Race is not*
> *to the swift nor the Battle to the Strong. Do you not think*
> *an Angel rides in the Whirlwind and directs this Storm?"*[77]

There was little doubt in the minds of most of the founding
fathers: they had achieved the impossible because God had won
the new republic *for* them.

They also understood that the ideas they were using to
build the new republic had also come from God. There is little
doubt they also mined pagan classical writers for ideas and
studied the political structure of ancient republics, but they
also knew that the ideas that worked best, the ones that stuck,
were the ones they derived from the Bible. Noah Webster, in his
history of America, wrote:

> *The brief exposition of the constitution of the United*
> *States, will unfold to young persons the principles of*
> *republican government; and it is the sincere desire of*

---

77   Quoted in Benson Bobrick, *Angel in the Whirlwind* (New York: Simon &
     Schuster America Collection, 1997), p. 186.

*the writer that our citizens should early understand
that the genuine source of correct republican principles
is the Bible.*[78]

The founders did not just see the hand of God at work in
the Revolutionary War; they also sensed His direction at the
Constitutional Convention, where they faced the impossible
task of pulling the hopes and aspirations of thirteen diverse
colonies under a single governmental structure with a unifying
vision. It was not an easy process, and the tempers of delegates
flared frequently; as hot as Independence Hall was the day they
gathered, the real heat was generated by disagreement. Half a
year after the Convention, James Madison expressed his shock
that it had worked at all:

*The real wonder is that so many difficulties should have
been surmounted, and surmounted with an unanimity
almost as unprecedented as it must have been unexpected. It is impossible for any man of candor to reflect
on this circumstance without partaking of the astonishment. It is impossible for the man of pious reflection not
to receive in it a finger of that Almighty hand which has
been so frequently and signally extended to our relief in
the critical stages of the revolution.*[79]

---

78 Noah Webster, *History of the United States,* Kindle locations 19-21, Kindle
   edition.

79 James Madison, "Federalist 37," in Robert Scigliano, ed., *The Federalist: A
   Commentary on the Constitution of the United States* (New York: Modern
   Library, 2001), p. 228.

This is not overstatement on the part of Madison. The Constitutional Convention nearly pulled apart at the seams when it came to how states would be represented at the federal level. Would each state receive an equal number of delegates, or would representation be based on the population of each state?[80]

It was a disagreement that nearly scuttled the entire exercise, until, on June 28, Benjamin Franklin suddenly stood up and began quoting Scripture to the assembly—by memory. Franklin himself was hardly what one would consider a traditional Christian. "I believe in one God, Creator of the Universe," he wrote to the president of Yale in 1790. "That He governs it by His Providence. That he ought to be worshipped. That the most acceptable Service we render to him, is doing Good to his other Children. That the Soul of Man is immortal, and will be treated with Justice in another Life respecting its Conduct in this. . . . As for Jesus of Nazareth . . . I think the system of Morals and Religion as he left them to us, the best the World ever saw . . . but I have . . . some Doubts to his Divinity; though it is a Question I do not dogmatism upon, having never studied it, and think it is needless to busy myself with it now, where I expect soon an Opportunity of knowing the Truth with less Trouble."[81]

While biblical Christians would bristle at his loose position on Christ's divinity, there is little question that Benjamin

---

80 To some extent, this debate continues to this day with regard to the Electoral College, in which delegates from each state help elect the president, based on the votes received state by state. In recent years, there have been voices insisting that it is time to abolish the College and elect a president based on national popular vote—a position that appears to ignore the hard-won balance established by the drafters of the Constitution.

81 Quoted in John Fea, "Religion And Early Politics: Benjamin Franklin and His Religious Beliefs," *Pennsylvania Heritage,* Fall 2011.

Franklin knew the contents of the Bible and considered the teachings of Christ a solid foundation for a just society. After quoting the Bible extensively, Franklin made an impassioned plea to the assembly:

> *"In the Situation of this Assembly, groping, as it were, in the dark to find Political Truth, and scarce able to distinguish it when presented to us, how has it happened, Sir, that we have not hitherto once thought of humbly applying to the Father of Lights to illuminate our Understandings? In the Beginning of the Contest with Britain, when we were sensible of Danger, we had daily Prayers in this Room for the Divine Protection. Our Prayers, Sir, were heard; —and they were graciously answered. All of us, who were engaged in the Struggle, must have observed frequent Instances of a superintending Providence in our Favor. To that kind Providence we owe this happy opportunity of consulting in peace on the means of establishing our future national felicity. And have we now forgotten that powerful Friend? or do we now imagine that we no longer need its assistance. I have lived, Sir, a long time, and the longer I live, the more convincing proofs I see of this Truth, that God governs in the affairs of men."*[82]

This was not just an expression of faith in a God who could save their national ambitions, but it was also an allusion to the book of Daniel, where God had demonstrated His sovereignty over the kingdoms of earth and had outlined the

---

82 Quoted in Daniel L. Dreisbach, *Reading the Bible with the Founding Fathers* (New York: Oxford University Press, 2017), p. 137.

course of world history in advance. Human history was not the product of mere chance, but was being orchestrated by the divine Hand. Many in the room agreed with Franklin: God had brought them thus far, and they could trust Him to see the project through to completion.

While many of the delegates were not what we would define as "born-again Christians," because some were skeptical that the *entire* Bible had been inspired by God, they all conceded that something special had obviously happened in the rise of their new nation. There was just no other way to explain it. Even Thomas Paine, a notorious critic of the Bible, still recognized the superiority of its moral principles for governing a society:

> *As the exalting one man so greatly above the rest cannot be justified on the equal rights of nature, so neither can it be defended on the authority of scripture; for the will of the Almighty, as declared by Gideon and the prophet Samuel, expressly disapproves of government by kings.*[83]

The difference between the French and American revolutions hinges on the importance given to an external, time-tested source of moral authority: in this case, the Bible. The French revolutionaries rejected it outright, associating it with the oppression they had experienced at the hands of the church-state alliance that had dominated Europe for so many centuries. In their haste to demolish existing hierarchical structures, they did not pause to ask why such structures were needed in the first place. (We see a similar, but slower, careless deconstruction

---

83   Thomas Paine, *Common Sense,* Kindle locations 133-135, Kindle edition.

of society taking place in our own world today. Those intent on erasing the past and thoughtlessly jettisoning every hierarchical structure that has held our civilization together wish to dispense with every historical reminder of where this nation has come from. This is described as "progress," although those who advocate such drastic social upheavals can seldom give a rational defense of what they think they are "progressing" toward, and seem unaware that nearly every such social upheaval in the past has pushed toward tyranny.)

The same can be said of the Bolshevik Revolution in 1917, where the time-tested social structures were suddenly pulled apart in an attempt to remedy injustice. The result? A regime that was much worse than the Tsars, which systematically murdered tens of millions of its own citizens until its collapse toward the end of the twentieth century.

But the American Revolution was different, and while the Revolutionary War was certainly devastating to countless families, the product of that revolution was essentially different from other less-careful attempts to overthrow the existing order. The founders *did* have a reverence for an outside, higher source of moral authority. They were keen students of the classics, of course—produced by civilizations that had already achieved greatness in the past—but above all, they respected the time-tested moral teachings of Scripture.

Thanks to their love for the Scriptures and their careful, thoughtful approach to deconstructing the monarchy under which they suffered, the early Americans proved to be a remarkably literate people. The great French observer and cheerleader of the American experiment, Alexis de Tocqueville, wrote that even the most humble American appeared

well-read and educated, in spite of the seemingly untamed
nature of the frontier:

> *Americans do not use the word peasant. They do not
> use the word because they do not possess the idea. The
> ignorance of primitive ages, the simplicity of the coun-
> tryside, the rusticity of the village—they have preserved
> none of these things and have no conception of the vir-
> tues or vices, the coarse habits, or the naive graces of a
> nascent civilization.*

> *At the outer reaches of the confederated states, where soci-
> ety and wilderness meet, there subsists a population of
> bold adventurers who, fleeing the poverty that lay ready
> to afflict them had they remained beneath their fathers'
> roofs, fearlessly braved America's solitudes in search of
> a new homeland. No sooner does the pioneer reach his
> chosen place of refuge than he chops down a few trees and
> builds a cabin in the woods. Nothing is more wretched to
> look at than one of these forlorn shacks. A traveler who
> draws near as dusk descends can see the flicker of the
> hearth through chinks in the walls, and at night, if the
> wind picks up, he can hear the rustle of the leafy roof min-
> gle with the other sounds of the forest. It is only natural to
> suppose that a cottage as poor as this must be home to
> coarse and ignorant people. Yet one must not assume that
> the pioneer in any way reflects the place he has chosen for
> an asylum. Everything around him is primitive and wild,
> but he is the product, so to speak, of eighteen centuries of
> effort and experience. He wears the clothes and speaks the*

language of the city. He knows the past, is curious about the future, and argues about the present. He is a highly civilized man who, having plunged into the wilds of the New World with his Bible, ax, and newspapers, has chosen to live for a time in the forest.[84]

This important observation flies in the face of the oft-repeated trope that biblical Christianity held the world in ignorance and superstition until the secular reasoning of the Enlightenment liberated us. It simply isn't true: the American founders were biblically literate and achieved the world's greatest political feat. They were not ignorant: they read widely, but framed an understanding of what they were reading with the moral principles enumerated in the Bible. They carefully used reason and informed it with faith.

The importance of this cannot be overstated, and it is one of the key differences between the French and American revolutions. When French revolutionaries rejected faith along with the power structures that had been oppressing them, they lost an important moral reference point that would have enabled them to build a much more stable and far less fearful republic. When you pull down an existing authority structure, it becomes important to have a superior system to put in its place; otherwise, you will merely replace the self-centered interests of monarchs and bishops with the self-centered interests of a mob.

"Woe to those who are wise in their own eyes," the prophet Isaiah wrote roughly two and a half millennia before either

---

84 Alexis de Tocqueville, *Democracy in America,* trans. Arthur Goldhammer (New York: Library of America, 2004), p. 350.

revolution, "and prudent in their own sight!" (Isaiah 5:21).
Without an external source of moral authority, human beings
will use their own interests as a guide to what is moral, creating
a situation where morality becomes essentially meaningless:

> Woe to those who call evil good, and good evil; who put
> darkness for light, and light for darkness; who put bitter
> for sweet, and sweet for bitter! Woe to those who are
> wise in their own eyes, and prudent in their own sight!
> (Isaiah 5:20, 21).

This is why the deep Reformation roots of the American Revolution proved so important, and the reason that it
is a mistake to assume that the American republic was first
and foremost a product of the Enlightenment. It was not;
the founders gleaned the best from both the pagan classics
and Enlightenment philosophers, of course, but their ideas
of what was wrong with monarchy were informed chiefly by
the Scriptures.

In fact, it has often been said that the architects of this
nation were so influenced by Scripture that many of the documents leading up to the Constitutional Convention read like
biblical documents:

> Following an extensive survey of American political
> literature from 1760 to 1805, political scientist Don-
> ald S. Lutz reported that the Bible was referenced
> more frequently than any European writer or even
> any European school of thought, such as the Enlight-
> enment or Whig intellectual traditions. Indeed the

Bible accounted for about one-third of all citations in his sample. According to Lutz, "Deuteronomy is the most frequently cited book, followed by Montesquieu's The Spirit of the Laws. *Biblical sources figured prominently in the study even though Lutz excluded from his sample most political pamphlets and tracts, including many political sermons, that had no citations to secular sources. This significantly undercounted biblical sources because "at least 80 percent of the political pamphlets during the 1770s and 1780s were written by ministers," and, yet, Lutz included in his sample "only about one-tenth of the reprinted sermons" (by contrast, the sample included "about one-third of all significant secular publications").*[85]

Writing to Benjamin Rush in 1807, John Adams stated:

"The Bible contains the most profound philosophy, the most perfect morality, and the most refined policy, that was ever conceived upon earth. It is the most republican book in the world, and therefore I will still revere it. . . . Without national morality a republican government cannot be maintained."[86]

Even Benjamin Franklin, a deist, expressed his admiration for the morality of the Scriptures:

---

85 Dreisbach, p. 2.

86 Quoted in ibid., p. 49.

*As to Jesus of Nazareth, I think his system of morals and
his religion, as he left them to us, the best the world ever
saw or is like to see.*[87]

The appeal to an external, higher moral authority, and to
the Bible in particular, is one of the secrets behind American
"exceptionalism." This is a term that has been grossly misunderstood by our current generation as an expression of arrogance—that Americans somehow believe themselves to be
intrinsically better human beings than their neighbors. That is
not what is meant. Neither does it mean that the United States
is simply unique or different. *Exceptionalism* implies something
more: that the birth of America was the product of destiny, a
forerunner of better ideals about to break upon the timeline of
human history.

And in this sense, she *was* exceptional: while casting
aside the tyranny of princes and prelates, she did not devolve
into anarchy, but appealed to a moral authority and rights that
derive directly from God Himself. "We hold these truths to be
self-evident," the Declaration of Independence reads, "that all
men are created equal, that they are endowed by their Creator
with certain unalienable Rights, that among these are Life, Liberty and the pursuit of Happiness."

The role of government was to *ensure* those rights. While it
seems obvious to us, it was a radical idea whose time had come.

---

87 Benjamin Franklin, letter to Ezra Stiles, 1790. You can find a copy of the
letter at: https://www.bartleby.com/400/prose/366.html. Franklin goes
on to doubt the divinity of Christ in the following sentences, but his
affirmation of biblical morality is indicative of those of the time who did
not necessarily hold to orthodox Christian beliefs, but recognized the
superiority of Judeo-Christian morality nonetheless.

The long-hoped-for dreams of English Dissidents had, in the New World, flourished into a reality—and it was something that had never been accomplished before. There had been other republics in the distant past, some of which were stable for a number of centuries, but never before had the rights of the *individual* before God been enshrined like this.

Furthermore, it would not be a democracy—or at least a *direct* democracy—but a republic. Democracies are notoriously unstable in the long run, because simple majorities can inflict the will of one segment of society on the others, or even void the rights of individuals and minorities. For this reason, democracies have long been criticized by any number of prominent thinkers—from Plato and Aristotle to Rousseau and Montesquieu—as being untenable for any length of time.

As has been famously stated (possibly by eighteenth-century professor Alexander Fraser Tytler[88]):

> *A democracy cannot exist as a permanent form of government. It can only exist until the voters discover that they can vote themselves largesse from the public treasury. From that moment on, the majority always votes for the candidates promising the most benefits from the public treasury with the result that a democracy always collapses over loose fiscal policy, always followed by a dictatorship.*

A republic would be different. It would use representational democracy, where each state and/or district would send representatives to the government, but the essential structures

---

88 This quote is usually attributed to Tytler, but a number of sources question that assumption, given that it appears in none of his published works.

and processes of government would be firmly entrenched in
a supreme written law. No one sect or political faction would
be able to overwhelm the system and create tyranny. In 1787,
James Madison wrote:

> *The influence of factious leaders may kindle a flame
> within their particular States, but will be unable to
> spread a general conflagration through the other States.
> A religious sect may degenerate into a political faction
> in a part of the Confederacy; but the variety of sects dis-
> persed over the entire face of it must secure the national
> councils against any danger from that source. A rage
> for paper money, for an abolition of debts, for an equal
> division of property, or for any other improper or wicked
> project, will be less apt to pervade the whole body of
> the Union than a particular member of it; in the same
> proportion as such a malady is more likely to taint a par-
> ticular county or district, than an entire State.*[89]

While in some ways resembling (and borrowing from)
successful republics and democracies of the ancient past,
what the founders created was quite unlike anything that had
ever been done before. It stood in the tradition of the Hebrew
republic, and was a deliberate effort to recapture what God had
originally set out as the best way to live. Mere months ahead of
the signing of the Declaration of Independence, John Adams
marveled at the unprecedented opportunity the founders had
to restructure human government from the ground up:

---

89   James Madison, "Federalist 10," in Scigliano.

"It has been the will of Heaven that we should be thrown into existence at a period when the greatest philosophers and lawgivers of antiquity would have wished to live. A period when [we have] an opportunity of beginning government anew from the foundation. . . . How few of the human race have ever had any opportunity of choosing a system of government for themselves and their children."[90]

In matters of faith and personal conviction, individual Americans would be directly answerable to God. There would be no need for a human monarch or bishop to serve as a mediator. Citizens would not be required to channel their prayers to the Almighty through the machinery of a state church, and they would not be required to worship the way the government demanded, as had happened in England (although the separation of church and state took a little while to sort out in a few localities).

It is in *this* sense that the United States is a Christian nation: it is not a political theocracy, where the state dictates faith; it is free, so that the individual can answer the call of conscience as he or she sees fit.

Unfortunately, we now live in a time when many appear to be ignorant of the origins of the legally-enforced liberties they enjoy, and there are still voices that occasionally cry out for the church to run the nation. Of course, what those voices mean is *their* church, and they are usually well-intentioned: they wish

---

90 Quoted in Jeremy Gunn et al., eds., *No Establishment of Religion: America's Original Contribution to Religious Liberty* (Oxford: Oxford University Press, 2012), p. 181.

to see a correction in the all-too-obvious downward spiral of public morality. But this is *not* the solution provided by the American Constitution. If there is to be revival, it must be *personal* revival; and if you wish to convince your neighbor of the merits of your faith, you must use persuasion, not legal coercion. While the nation has clearly been built on the principles of Scripture, those biblical principles have produced a republic in which "because the Bible says so" will never be an argument for new legislation.

In 1785, James Madison dramatically underscored the age-old problem with allowing the church to hold the reins of government and the reason that it would not be permitted in the new republic:

> *Torrents of blood have been spilt in the old world, by vain attempts of the secular arm, to extinguish Religious discord, by proscribing all difference in Religious opinion. Time has at length revealed the true remedy. Every relaxation of narrow and rigorous policy, wherever it has been tried, has been found to assuage the disease.*[91]

There would be checks on power in this new republic, because human beings, historically, have seldom been able to exercise unbridled power ethically or to the advantage of the governed. The "benevolent dictator," that canard of political theory, was a myth, and no such situation would be permitted in the United States. If the church were able to put a bit in the

---

91 James Madison, "Memorial and Remonstrance against Religious Assessments," 1785, par. 11, https://founders.archives.gov/documents/Madison/01-08-02-0163.

mouth of the state, as it did in Europe after Constantine, the American republic would reproduce the horrors that ensued. In that world, people died for holding the "wrong" opinion. In America, you could hold any opinion you wanted.

The answer, the founders asserted, would be to keep Caesar from entering the church, and the church from answering to Caesar. The most diverse religious beliefs would be able to coexist peacefully. J. Hector St. John de Crèvecoeur, a famous writer of the time, said in amazement, "All sects are mixed, as well as all nations; thus religious indifference is imperceptibly disseminated from one end of the continent to the other, which is at present of the strongest characteristics of the Americans."[92]

In 1790, shortly after the ratification of the Constitution, members of a Hebrew synagogue in Rhode Island, who instinctively understood that America had been born as a *Christian* nation, became worried that the problems Jews had faced in the Old World would repeat themselves in the new. In August, George Washington wrote them a letter to set their minds at ease. It is worth reproducing in full, because it underscores the spirit of the day:

Gentlemen.

While I receive, with much satisfaction, your Address replete with expressions of affection and esteem; I rejoice in the opportunity of assuring you, that I shall always retain a grateful remembrance of the cordial welcome I experienced in my visit to Newport, from all classes of Citizens.

---

92 Quoted in Jon Meacham, *American Gospel: God, the Founding Fathers, and the Making of a Nation* (New York: Random House, 2006), p. 91.

The reflection on the days of difficulty and danger which are past is rendered the more sweet, from a consciousness that they are succeeded by days of uncommon prosperity and security. If we have wisdom to make the best use of the advantages with which we are now favored, we cannot fail, under the just administration of a good Government, to become a great and a happy people.

The Citizens of the United States of America have a right to applaud themselves for having given to mankind examples of an enlarged and liberal policy: a policy worthy of imitation. All possess alike liberty of conscience and immunities of citizenship. It is now no more that toleration is spoken of, as if it was by the indulgence of one class of people, that another enjoyed the exercise of their inherent natural rights. For happily the Government of the United States, which gives to bigotry no sanction, to persecution no assistance requires only that they who live under its protection should demean themselves as good citizens, in giving it on all occasions their effectual support.

It would be inconsistent with the frankness of my character not to avow that I am pleased with your favorable opinion of my Administration, and fervent wishes for my felicity. May the Children of the Stock of Abraham, who dwell in this land, continue to merit and enjoy the good will of the other Inhabitants; while every one shall sit in safety under his own vine and figtree, and there shall be none to make him afraid. May the father of all

mercies scatter light and not darkness in our paths, and
make us all in our several vocations useful here, and in
his own due time and way everlastingly happy.

G. Washington[93]

The "vine and figtree" line was a quote from the Old Testament, where God describes His ideal kingdom, where the diverse peoples of the earth live in peace before Him:

Many nations shall come and say, "Come, and let us go
up to the mountain of the Lord, to the house of the God
of Jacob; He will teach us His ways, and we shall walk in
His paths." For out of Zion the law shall go forth, and the
word of the Lord from Jerusalem. He shall judge between
many peoples, and rebuke strong nations afar off; they
shall beat their swords into plowshares, and their spears
into pruning hooks; nation shall not lift up sword against
nation, neither shall they learn war anymore. But every-
one shall sit under his vine and under his fig tree, and no
one shall make them afraid; for the mouth of the Lord of
hosts has spoken. For all people walk each in the name
of his god, but we will walk in the name of the Lord our
God forever and ever (Micah 4:2–5).

The American experiment was remarkably successful. There is little question that it was populated by people as imperfect as any generation that lived before them. There have been notable

---

93 You can find this letter at: https://founders.archives.gov/documents/
    Washington/05-06-02-0135.

shortcomings in the implementation of America's constitutional ideals—not the least of which was a failure to immediately eliminate the reprehensible practice of slavery.[94] But what the founders produced, while standing on the shoulders of the Dissenters, was spectacular. Never before in the history of the world had there been such a daring experiment in self-government, and it produced the freest—and eventually, the most powerful and wealthiest—nation in the history of the world.

The American colossus looms so large on the horizon of human history, and its appearance seems so improbable, that the question must be asked: did the biblical prophets not anticipate such a startling development? If the founders of this nation were correct in their conviction that God had helped them establish this nation, shouldn't we be able to find it in prophecy? If Babylon and Rome were there, why not the most powerful nation in human history?

It *is* there, but it is not immediately obvious.

You'll remember from earlier in this study that the Old Testament prophet Daniel predicted the history of world empires centuries before they arrived on the scene:

In Daniel 2, God showed this history to Nebuchadnezzar using a statue to represent successive world empires, from Babylon to Rome. The toes of the statue anticipated the breakup of the Western Roman Empire and the rise of Western European nations.

---

94 In 1790, not long after the Constitutional Convention, two Quaker
    delegations appealed to the House to abolish the slave trade, but in an
    effort to keep southern states at the table, the subject was deliberately
    kicked down the road. Seven decades would pass before America finally
    faced this inconsistency in the painful throes of the Civil War.

In the seventh chapter, Daniel witnesses the same progression of empires, but this time, instead of using a statue, God presents the same history—in advance—by showing him a series of animals rising up out of the Gentile sea. (See Chapter 4.)

It is this second vision, involving the beasts from the sea, to which we need to turn our attention. Careful students of the Bible have noticed that these four animals—a winged lion, a bear, a four-winged leopard, and a fearsome beast—correspond directly to the body parts of the odd conglomerate beast that appears in Revelation 13:

> *Then I stood on the sand of the sea. And I saw a beast rising up out of the sea, having seven heads and ten horns, and on his horns ten crowns, and on his heads a blasphemous name. Now the beast which I saw was like a leopard, his feet were like the feet of a bear, and his mouth like the mouth of a lion. The dragon gave him his power, his throne, and great authority* (Revelation. 13:1, 2).

The similarity is obviously not a coincidence; both John and Daniel are trying to tell us something important. In Daniel's version the beasts remain separate from each other, because they were still in the future. But more than six centuries later John saw them mashed together in a grotesque single animal. The Gentile kingdoms had all come and gone, and he was living under Roman domination—the fourth beast of Daniel's vision.

That fourth beast, as we have seen, had ten horns on its head, pointing forward to the collapse of the Western Empire, and then a "little horn" that emerged among them. Throughout the centuries, diligent scholars have realized that this eleventh horn is none other than the misguided marriage of church and state that emerged on the ruins of the former Roman Empire: it is an embarrassing depiction of *us*. Just as God's Old Testament people had demanded a human king and then subsequently abandoned the terms of their covenant with the Creator, the New Testament church had compromised with the Roman Empire to devastating effect.

As the church filled the power vacuum left behind by the implosion of Rome, we became more political than moral.

The little horn of Daniel 7 proves to be one and the same thing as the strange conglomerate beast of Revelation 13; the descriptions, from its boastful claims and the length of its rule to its persecuting nature, match perfectly. John is showing us that the politicized church, with its human power struc-tures, is the final and ultimate manifestation of human efforts to govern this planet apart from God. The church of the Western Empire is the heir to all the Gentile kingdoms that came before it, and it is the ultimate expression of arrogant human kingship. It not only commands political power over the nations of the world, but demands worship as well; it is a tragic marriage of church and state:

> And he was given a mouth speaking great things and blasphemies, and he was given authority to continue for forty-two months. Then he opened his mouth in blas-phemy against God, to blaspheme His name, His taber-nacle, and those who dwell in heaven. It was granted to him to make war with the saints and to overcome them. And authority was given him over every tribe, tongue, and nation (Revelation 13:5–7).

This religious-political beast power, however, does not work alone. Later in the same chapter a *second* beast appears, and this beast makes it his business to give the first beast what it wants: the compulsory worship of the world:

> And he exercises all the authority of the first beast in his presence, and causes the earth and those who dwell in it to worship the first beast, whose deadly wound was healed. He performs great signs, so that he even makes fire come down from heaven on the earth in the sight of men. And he deceives those who dwell on the earth—by those signs which he was granted to do in the sight of the beast, telling those who dwell on the earth to make an image to the beast who was wounded by the sword and lived. He was granted power to give breath to the image of the beast, that the image of the beast should both speak and cause as many as would not worship the image of the beast to be killed (Revelation 13:12–15).

It is important to study the details surrounding these beasts carefully.[95] There is important context in the previous chapter, where John sees the dragon, who gives the first beast his throne,[96] persecuting the "woman," or God's people:

> So the serpent spewed water out of his mouth like a flood after the woman, that he might cause her to be carried away by the flood (Revelation 12:15).

---

95 Even more carefully than we are able to in a short book like this. This line of study will prove well worth your time.

96 Revelation 13:2.

It is describing the tragic reality of medieval Europe: those who wished to distance themselves from the official church-state of the former Roman Empire found themselves being relentlessly persecuted. Throughout the centuries, some have estimated that as many as 50 million people were put to death, not for actual crimes, but for matters of conscience. Those deemed "heretics" had their property confiscated, their rights proscribed, and ultimately faced the torture chamber or the stake for their beliefs. The embarrassment of our un-Christlike behavior during this period is common knowledge—everybody knows what "the Inquisition" is.

The beast from the sea in Revelation 13 fits this descrip-tion perfectly: it is a Gentile kingdom (another beast from the Gentile sea) with religious ambitions (the marriage of church and state in Europe), and it makes "war with the saints."[97] In Revelation 12, this persecution is shown as a devastating flood emanating from the mouth of the dragon.

And then something miraculous happens: just when it seems as if the woman would be "carried away by the flood," the earth suddenly opens up:

> *But the earth helped the woman, and the earth opened*
> *its mouth and swallowed up the flood which the dragon*
> *had spewed out of his mouth* (Revelation 12:16).

Did it happen? Absolutely. The earth quite literally opened up when Christopher Columbus suddenly discovered a place where people could escape the stifling religious restrictions of the Old

---

97 Revelation 13:7.

World. Prior to the fifteenth century, readers would have puzzled over the possible meanings of this passage, but in the wake of Columbus' discovery, the persecuted masses of Europe suddenly realized they didn't have to stay in Europe, forever subject to the whims of monarchs: they now had a place to go. New World colonies provided ample opportunity to build new, unhindered religious communities where people could live as they pleased.

The discovery of the Americas was a divine remedy to the problems posed by Daniel's little horn and John's megalomaniacal sea beast, and this New World would witness the birth of a republic where the principles of religious liberty found in Scripture would finally be a reality.

And if that were the end of the story, we could say, "They all lived happily ever after"—but it isn't. There is a second beast, and he comes up *out of the earth*—the same place the persecuted masses of Europe fled to in order to find freedom:

> *Then I saw another beast coming up out of the earth, and he had two horns like a lamb and spoke like a dragon. And he exercises all the authority of the first beast in his presence, and causes the earth and those who dwell in it to worship the first beast, whose deadly wound was healed* (Revelation 13:11, 12).

This "earth" beast is another political power, like the first, and it rises in the New World. It looks like a lamb but speaks like a dragon. You'll also notice that the first beast has crowns on its horns, representing the monarchies of Europe; this second beast has no crowns. Why? It is a republic. Throughout the book of Revelation a lamb represents Christ.[98] A dragon represents Satan,[99] the instigator of religious persecution.

This is the point where America makes her grand appearance in the pages of Bible prophecy, and it is mixed news. She would, at first, appear Christlike, established on biblical principles—but then eventually she will become just like every other empire in the history of the world: a coercive abuser of power. America will speak with the voice of the dragon, the same dragon that gave the first beast its power and authority in the Old World. Even worse, she will drive the *whole world* back to the first beast, forcing us back to the unholy alliance between church and state that caused people to flee the Old World in the first place.

The identity of this second beast was recognized by a handful of Christians well before the Declaration of Independence was signed. In the throes of the Great Awakening, a revival that swept across the American continent (and continued in a second wave well into the nineteenth century), Ebenezer Frothingham, the pastor of a church in Wethersfield, Connecticut, was arrested and imprisoned for preaching without permission. He recognized the potential for the colonies to devolve into the same type of religious authoritarianism that had existed in Europe.

Indignant that his God-given religious liberty had been violated, he wrote:

> If that Beast which hath two Horns like a Lamb, and speaks as a Dragon, has no rule in this Land, we enquire, then, Whence it is that the Saints of God have been so imprisoned of late Years, who did their fellow

---

98   See, for example, Revelation 5:12, 13.

99   See Revelation 12:9.

Men no wrong, nor was they guilty of the Breach of any moral Precept that is to be punished by Man; but on the contrary, endeavouring in the Fear of God, and Order of the Gospel, to seek and promote the best Peace, Good, and Happiness of their fellow Men? Some have been haled before Rulers, and to Prison, for nothing else but preaching the Gospel of Jesus Christ. The very Face of their Complaints, or Charge laid against them was nothing more criminal than this, that they had preached the Gospel so and so, which was contrary to the Laws of this Colony. . . .

What Power is that which hath imprisoned the Saints for not attending and supporting that Worship which they know by God's Word and Spirit, is not according to Divine Appointment, but contrary to the plain Letter of the Word of God?[100]

The republic had yet to be born, and this influential preacher already recognized the potential for human beings to repeat their age-old mistakes in the New World. Old World ideas about state control of the church lingered in the memories of colonists, some of whom didn't mind using them if it meant *their* religious ideas were preferred. America, Frothingham noted, would be the second beast.

It is not hard to see how more than two centuries of existence have helped many Americans forget from whence they came

---

100 Ebenezer Frothingham, *A Discourse upon the great Privileges of the Church of Jesus Christ*, in Alan Heimert et al., eds., *The Great Awakening* (New York: Bobbs-Merrill Company, 1967), pp. 452, 453.

and why the republic exists. In recent decades, there has been a noticeable shift in the culture of the nation. It is no longer obvious to some that the United States is the brightest beacon of freedom on earth. We have discovered that the National Security Administration listens to our phone calls and intercepts our emails. We have seen interest groups suddenly audited by the IRS when government officials do not like what they have to say. We have witnessed the government violating personal religious liberty in order to bolster a mandatory government program.

It is no longer 1776, and the crucial ideas that burned so brightly in the hearts of the founders have faded into the background of twenty-first-century life in America, where it is doubtful that most citizens could name more than one or two of the signers of the Declaration of Independence. We are no longer conversant in the political philosophies that gave birth to our liberties, and few people remember that the Judeo-Christian Scriptures played such an indispensable role in the birth of the nation.

In the great timeline of Bible prophecy, we find ourselves perched on the head of a beast that is quickly shifting from lamb to dragon. Our biggest problem today is not that the nation has become secular and postmodern, although it is certainly disheartening for Bible-believing Christians to watch so many of their fellow Americans abandon the faith that provided them with the liberties they enjoy.

No, the bigger problem is the growing ignorance of how and why this republic has been structured as it is. If we forget *why* the founders created what they did, we will more easily regress into the world we once left and throw the rights of our neighbors under the bus if it seems expedient for our own well-being. Words like *honor, duty,* and *character* are fading from public discourse, and where we once believed in something bigger than ourselves, we have begun to question whether or not America was worth establishing in the first place.

It is a precarious situation we find ourselves in. Without a sense of the transcendent, without an appeal to a higher, external source of morality, devotion to principle can become very weak in the face of a crisis. The temptation to surrender God-given liberties in order to create a sense of personal security can be overpowering; it has happened many times in history. Should the American people deconstruct the Constitution or turn a blind eye to it, something very rare in the course of human history, liberty, will have been lost.

It cost us far too much to get here to throw it away suddenly, but it seems that we are determined to throw it away at any rate. We see social media platforms such as Facebook and Twitter bowing to public cries to censor certain political perspectives.[101] Where colleges and universities were once paragons of diverse expression, speakers deemed controversial by small groups of agitators are now prevented from making appearances for the sake of making students feel "safe."[102] If

---

101 Social media platforms, of course, are privately owned and thus not covered by the First Amendment, which prevents *government* from interfering with free expression. They are no more required to keep your account open than you are required to keep an unwelcome guest in your home. But given the incredibly broad reach of such platforms, the trend toward censorship is worrisome, because it reflects a broader trend to silence dissent in the public sphere.

102 Notoriously, former Secretary of State Condoleezza Rice was pressured in 2014 to step down as the commencement speaker at Rutgers University because protesters didn't like her involvement in the Iraq War. In the past, it would have been unthinkable to forcibly silence our nation's most powerful influencers because of ideological differences.

they *do* make it to a campus, it is not uncommon for protesters to disrupt the event sufficiently that those who *would* like
to hear the speaker are ultimately denied that right.

This is *not* the America the founders envisioned. Nor is it
the America Madison wrote about, where sectarian groups were
never to be granted sufficient power to trample the God-given
liberties of their neighbors. It is true that the First Amendment,
which guarantees that Congress cannot pass laws "abridging
the freedom of speech . . . or the right of the people peaceably to
assemble," was designed to ensure that *government* could never
silence dissent—but the trend toward censorship is worrisome
in that it is never far from a cultural trend to a bill on the floor
of the House.

Granted, understanding how the rights enumerated in the
eighteenth century apply to life in the twenty-first century is
not always easy territory to navigate. Shouldn't my neighbor's
opinion be legally silenced if he is an anti-Semite and I am a
Jew? If the presidential candidate with the most *popular* votes
loses the Electoral College, shouldn't we move to a direct
democracy? If someone in my family is injured or killed by a
firearm, shouldn't we consider repealing the Second Amendment? Should Catholic nuns be forced to provide birth control
to their employees in order to expedite the implementation of a
national healthcare program that many people want? Should a
baker be forced to create wedding cakes for same-sex marriages
if it runs contrary to his religious conscience?

These have proven to be contentious questions fraught
with strong emotion, regardless of your personal ideology. But
because of the way the nation was founded, the answer to each
of these must be *no*: we cannot abridge the constitutionally

guaranteed rights of others because we do not like their position, and we cannot compel people to act in violation of their
sincerely held religious beliefs.[103] We cannot abridge our neighbor's rights simply because our neighbor makes us squirm. We
do not have a right to never be offended or never hear something we do not wish to hear; we each have the right to live by
the dictates of our conscience.

If we do not defend someone else's right to disagree with
us, no matter how distasteful we find his or her position, we
will find ourselves walking a very short road to losing our own
rights, because it will not be long until someone who finds *our*
beliefs reprehensible will attempt to silence us. Remember:
history is replete with those who deemed Christianity to be
objectionable. In places where freedom of expression has been
curtailed by the government, and where that government is
highly centralized and ideological, the preaching of the gospel
has frequently been curtailed or forbidden. When the people
start serving the state instead of the other way around, the
rights of the many will be trampled under the priorities of a
few, because those who hold power frequently view contrary
opinions as barriers to their own ambitions.

The American experiment is a rare enough phenomenon
in the long arc of human history that we simply cannot afford
to take our liberty for granted. Today, many other nations have

---

103 There is another recent case that differs somewhat from the others—a
   clerk who refused to issue same-sex marriage licenses. The baker owned
   his bakery; she did not own the county office and was hired to carry
   out a government function. In America, reasonable accommodation for
   religious beliefs is required, and perhaps the county office could have
   removed her from that responsibility, or perhaps she should have simply
   found other employment.

adopted many of the democratic principles established by the founders, so it is easy to fall under the illusion that life has always been this free. It has not, and historically, free people have not remained free for long. As author and historian Curtis McManus states, "We desire to see Roman ruins—but we do not desire to listen to them, for we assume that they have nothing to say. But such are the consequences of living in a culture in which the past is presented as nothing more than ignorance and criminality."[104]

Indeed. In our haste to deconstruct the American republic and raise something else on its ruins (whatever that is), we have been working under the assumption that our past was a mistake. We jettison everything and anything if we can find *anything* negative attached to it. Our grasp of history, philosophy, and religion has slipped into woeful disrepair, and like the Jacobins of France, we are destroying for the sake of destroying, without being fully aware of *what* we are demolishing.

The democratic experiments of antiquity eventually collapsed into tyranny, and we would be foolish to think that it could never happen to us. Selfish human nature is a stubborn fact of history, and should the checks and balances against the abuse of power be removed, it will happen again. Indeed, we have already been told that the lamb *will* speak like a dragon.

It is true that America is far from perfect, and it never has been perfect. We are, after all, a nation of sinners who, if unchecked by the power and influence of the gospel, will seek self above all. After all, slavery continued for seven decades

---

104 Curtis R. McManus, *The Age of Nihilism: An Inquiry into the Death of Western Democracy or, The Consequences of Philosophy* (FriesenPress), Kindle edition.

after the ratification of the Constitution, and in the face of a Declaration of Independence that guaranteed life, liberty, and the pursuit of happiness to everyone. And even after abolition, Jim Crow laws continued to make a mockery of our professed love for equality. It is to our embarrassment that it took so long to recognize that women have the right to vote, that right finally being entrenched in the Constitution in 1920. The treatment of Native Americans during our westward expansion was horrific.

Today, lobbyists and special interest groups seem to be able to buy decisions in Washington, to the point where pundits have joked that politicians should be required to wear sponsor stickers like race cars. In the middle of the twentieth century, MK-Ultra conducted experiments with hallucinogenic drugs on unsuspecting citizens. We have sterilized and lobotomized people against their will.

No, America is far from perfect. It is easy to catalog a long list of her sins. But what we have in this nation is still worth fighting for. The founders were not trying to establish utopia;[105] they were constructing a system in which very imperfect people could live freely, side by side. The Constitution is a document that recognizes human fallenness and imperfection; it is, after all, largely a set of guardrails to prevent abuse of power—which would not be necessary if utopia were really possible.

The American Constitution deals with human beings as they *are*, and as they always have been, not as we might hope they will be at some unknown point in the distant future. It is

---

105 By contrast, many who now wish to deconstruct America seem to hold out the promise of a future utopia where evil has been systematically rooted out and human nature has been essentially changed.

firmly grounded in reality, and it is to the credit of Americans that they have almost always addressed violations of liberty. Slowly, perhaps, and sometimes inadequately, but they did it—precisely because the structure allows it.

The *ideas* that gave birth to this republic were right. The biblical foundations of those ideas are solid. They are worth fighting for, for as long as we can cling to them. The other alternatives, short of the second coming of Christ, are not pretty. Since the birth of America, Marxists, National Socialists, and other tyrants have constructed horrific slaughter mills that led to the death of tens of millions. Europe, under the thumb of a state church, was not a pleasant place to live. On this side of glory, there has never been anything quite as conducive to liberty as the United States of America.

Of course, it is still a human system of government, even though it was built on biblical principles, and as such it will eventually fail. *All* human governments will fail. The prophecies of Daniel and Revelation make it abundantly clear that our only hope is the coming of the kingdom of Christ. The governments we've built, the empires we've praised, all of them end up on the trash heap of history the moment Jesus returns:

> *Then the seventh angel sounded: And there were loud voices in heaven, saying, "The kingdoms of this world have become the kingdoms of our Lord and of His Christ, and He shall reign forever and ever!"* (Revelation 11:15).

We are ultimately incapable of righting the wrongs that fell on the earth the moment we rebelled against its Creator. Every generation since then has learned the painful lesson that *no* human government, no matter how well-intentioned, is able to solve our worst problems. We are simply incapable of correcting fallen human nature, and every ideological effort to do so has failed miserably.

As we wait for Christ to come, we must never forget: this is earth's final empire. There is no successor mentioned in the Scriptures, apart from the kingdom of God. As Christians, our task is to preach the gospel to every nation, kindred, tongue, and people[106]—and America has genuinely provided the world with the best platform for accomplishing this. The ingenuity and creativity of the American people has blessed the world with the most powerful tools of mass communication in the history of the world, and—for the time being—the freedom to use them.

I have lived in places where we may *not* say what we wish on the airwaves, or print whatever we desire. America is not like that. Not yet.

So fight for her we must. Christians must do what they can to slow the inevitable transition from lamb to dragon so that we can faithfully accomplish the task that God has set before His church. To shamelessly appropriate and reinterpret the words of Dylan Thomas:

> *Do not go gentle into that good night,*
> *Old age should burn and rave at close of day;*
> *Rage, rage against the dying of the light.*

There is an incredible story found in the notes of Dr. James McHenry of Maryland, the youngest delegate to the Constitutional

---

106 Revelation 14:6; cf. Matthew 24:14, Acts 1:8.

Convention.[107] (Benjamin Franklin was the oldest.) As Benjamin Franklin exited the building at the end of the day, Mrs. Powell of Philadelphia approached him and asked, "Well, Doctor, what have we got? A republic or a monarchy?"

"A republic," replied the Doctor, "if you can keep it."

Indeed.

---

107 You can find his notes at: https://avalon.law.yale.edu/18th_century/ mchenry.asp. The story is also recounted in Eric Metaxas, *If You Can Keep It: The Forgotten Promise of American Liberty* (New York: Viking, 2016), p. 9.

Afterword

We have moved far too quickly, covering far more history and biblical material than is responsible for such a weighty topic. In some ways I have done it an injustice. What you have read is but the tip of the iceberg; a world of astonishment awaits you as you continue to dig into the prophecies of the Bible. If you have been given this book as part of an event, those who gave it to you are prepared to equip you for more study. If you have come across this book by some other means, you may request free Bible study guides through the Voice of Prophecy by writing to Box 999, Loveland, Colorado 80539, or by visiting www.vop.com/study.

Bibliography

Andress, David. *1789: The Threshold of the Modern Age*. New York: Farrar, Straus and Girous, 2008.

Bainton, Roland, ed. *Concerning Heretics by Sebastian Castellio*. New York: Octagon Books, 1979.

Berkin, Carol. *The Bill of Rights: The Fight to Secure America's Liberties*. New York: Simon & Schuster, 2015.

Blakely, William Addison. *American State Papers Bearing On Sunday Legislation*. New York: The National Religious Liberty Association, 1891.

Bobrick, Benson. *Angel in the Whirlwind*. New York: Simon & Schuster America Collection, 1997.

Brownworth, Lars. *Lost to the West*. New York: Crown Publishers, 2010.

Bunyan, John. *The Ruin of Antichrist*. Swengel, PA: Reiner Publications, 1970.

Castellio, Sebastian. *Advice to a Desolate France*. Grand Rapids, MI: Acton Institute, 2016.

Chinard, Gilbert. *Thomas Jefferson: The Apostle of Americanism*. Ann Arbor: University of Michigan Press, 1957.

Cliff, Nigel. *The Last Crusade: The Epic Voyages of Vasco da Gama*. New York: Harper Perennial, 2011.

Davidson, Miles H. *Columbus Then and Now: A Life Reexamined*. Norman, OK: University of Oklahoma Press, 1997.

De Tocqueville, Alexis. *Democracy in America*, trans. Arthur Goldhammer. New York: Library of America, 2004.

Delaney, Carol. *Columbus and the Quest for Jerusalem: How Religion Drove the Voyages that Led to America*. New York: Free Press, 2012.

Douthat, Ross. *Bad Religion: How We Became a Nation of Heretics*. New York: Free Press, 2012.

Dreisbach, Daniel L. *Reading the Bible with the Founding Fathers*. New York: Oxford University Press, 2017.

Ellis, Joseph. *Founding Brothers*. New York: Vintage Books, 2000.

Fleet, Kate. *European and Islamic Trade in the Early Ottoman State*. New York: Cambridge University Press, 2001.

Franklin, Benjamin. *The Autobiography and other Writings*. New York: Penguin Books, 1986.

Gibbon, Edward. *The History of the Decline and Fall of the Roman Empire*. New York: Kelmscott Society Publishers, 5 vols., 1845.

Grayling, A. C. *Toward the Light of Liberty: The Struggles for Freedom and Rights That Made the Modern Western World.* New York: Walker Publishing Co., 2007.

Greaves, Richard. *John Bunyan and English Nonconformity.* London: Hambledon Press, 1992.

Gunn, Jeremy et al., eds. *No Establishment of Religion: America's Original Contribution to Religious Liberty.* Oxford: Oxford University Press, 2012.

Heimert, Alan et al., eds. *The Great Awakening.* New York: Bobbs-Merrill Company, 1967.

Hinckley, Clark B. *Christopher Columbus: A Man among the Gentiles.* Salt Lake City: Deseret Books, 2014.

Hobbes, Thomas. *Leviathan.* Markham, Ontario: Penguin Books Canada, 1985.

Irving, Washington. *History of the Life and Voyages of Christopher Columbus.* LEEAF.com Classics. Kindle edition.

Lillback, Peter A. *George Washington's Sacred Fire.* Bryn Mawr, PA: Providence Forum Press, 2006.

Locke, John. *A Letter Concerning Toleration,* ed. James Tully. Indianapolis: Hackett Publishing Company, 1983.

Locke, John. *Second Treatise of Government,* ed. C. B. Macpherson. Indianapolis: Hackett Publishing Company, 1980.

Loconte, Joseph. *God, Locke, and Liberty.* New York: Lexington Books, 2014.

McManus, Curtis R. *The Age of Nihilism: An Inquiry into the Death of Western Democracy or, The Consequences of Philosophy.* Victoria, Canada: FriesenPress, 2018.

Meacham, Jon. *American Gospel: God, the Founding Fathers, and the Making of a Nation.* New York: Random House, 2006.

Medved, Michael. *The American Miracle: Divine Providence in the Rise of the Republic.* New York: Crown Forum, 2016.

Metaxas, Eric. *If You Can Keep It: The Forgotten Promise of American Liberty.* New York: Viking, 2016.

Milbrandt, Jay. *They Came For Freedom: The Forgotten, Epic Adventure of the Pilgrims.* Nashville: Nelson Books, 2017.

Nelson, Eric. *The Hebrew Republic: Jewish Sources and the Transformation of European Political Thought.* Cambridge: Harvard University Press, 2010.

Orgel, Stephen and Jonathan Goldberg, eds. *John Milton: The Major Works.* Oxford: Oxford University Press, 2008.

Padgett, JoAnn et al., eds. *The U.S. Constitution and Other Key American Writings*. San Diego: Word Cloud Classics, 2015.

Penn, William. *The Great Case of Liberty of Conscience Once More Briefly Debated & Defended*. Reproduction by EEBO Editions. Originally published 1670.

Philbrick, Nathaniel. *Mayflower: A Story of Courage, Community, and War*. New York: Penguin Group, 2007.

Quinn, David B. "Columbus and the North: England, Iceland, and Ireland." *The William and Mary Quarterly*, vol. 49, no. 2, 1992, pp. 278–297. http://www.jstor.org/stable/2947273.

Read, Piers Paul. *The Templars*. Cambridge, MA: Ca Capo Press, 1999.

Rugoff, Milton, ed. *The Travels of Marco Polo*. New York: Signet Classics, 1961.

Rusconi, Roberto, ed. *The Book of Prophecies Edited by Christopher Columbus*. Eugene, OR: Wipf and Stock Publishers, 1997.

Russell, Jeffrey Burton. *Inventing the Flat Earth: Columbus and Modern Historians*. Westport, CT: Praeger Publishers, 1997.

Scigliano, Robert, ed. *The Federalist: A Commentary on the Constitution of the United States*. New York: Modern Library, 2001.

Seneca. *Medea & Thyestes*. LRP. Kindle edition.

Spence-Jones, H. D. M. et al., eds. *The Pulpit Commentary*. New York: Funk & Wagnalls Company, 1909.

Thatcher, Oliver J. and Edgar Holmes McNeal, eds. *A Source Book for Mediæval History*. New York: Charles Scribner's Sons, 1905.

Vernon, Jamie L. "Understanding the Butterfly Effect." *American Scientist,* May–June 2017.

Waldman, Steven. *Founding Faith: How Our Founding Fathers Forged a Radical New Approach to Religious Liberty*. New York: Random House, 2009.

Waldman, Steven. *Sacred Liberty: America's Long, Bloody, and Ongoing Struggle for Religious Freedom*. New York: HarperOne, 2019.

West, Delno C. et al., trans. *The Libro de las profecias of Christopher Columbus*. Gainesville: University of Florida Press, 1991.